OUR

DIVINE

IDENTITY

T0017575

JOSHUA SAVAGE

OUR

DIVINE

IDENTITY

JOSHUA SAVAGE

CFI
An imprint of Cedar Fort, Inc.
Springville, Utah

This is not an official publication of The Church of Jesus Christ of Latter-day Saints. The opinions and views expressed herein belong solely to the author and do not necessarily represent the opinions or views of Cedar Fort, Inc. Permission for the use of sources, graphics, and photos is also solely the responsibility of the author.

ISBN 13: 978-1-4621-4494-5

Published by CFI, an imprint of Cedar Fort, Inc.
2373 W. 700 S., Suite 100, Springville, UT 84663
Distributed by Cedar Fort, Inc., www.cedarfort.com

Library of Congress Control Number: 2022950663

Cover design by Courtney Proby
Cover design © 2023 Cedar Fort, Inc.

Printed in the United States of America

10 9 8 7 6 5 4 3 2 1

Printed on acid-free paper

CONTENTS

ACKNOWLEDGMENTS

This work grew out of my doctoral studies at the University of Southern California on identity under the direction of Professor Eko Canillas. The course focus on identity did much to prompt me to review what the Lord had been revealing all along through His prophets.

As in all things, I am indebted to a loving and tutoring Lord who leads me along. I am also indebted to a small but mighty set of proof-readers who set aside valuable time to humor my writing pursuits. To Jon and Jane Anderson, P. Jeff Mulitalo, Sarit Catchatoorian, and Jennifer Savage I owe a special debt, as their early feedback and encouragement always does much to spur me along. As in previous works, the final copy benefited from the fine copyedit skills of David Nielson. To all involved, I extend my gratitude.

INTRODUCTION

This book is for people who have questions, who struggle to make sense of current events and the Lord's commandments. However, it is not intended to be definitive. Rather, it is an attempt to encourage those with questions to not make up their minds too quickly. It is an invitation to change your mind about what you think you know—an opportunity to acknowledge that while we believe "all that God has revealed," we also know that "He will yet reveal" so much more. We must, therefore, give heed to His words. This book attempts to help us in this endeavor.

Imagine you were invited by a friend to be present on April 6, 1830, at the small home of Peter Whitmer Sr. in rural upper state New York, where Joseph Smith organized the Church of Christ—as the Church was initially called—in the presence of at least thirty people.[1] You came because you heard that Joseph, a twenty-four-year-old farmer, had been given authority from God to reorganize His Church upon the earth. "By unanimous vote" all present "voted to accept and sustain Joseph Smith Jr. and Oliver Cowdery as the presiding officers of the Church."[2] This you did by a raise of the hand. Afterward, Joseph Smith instructed you and the others gathered as follows: "Wherefore, meaning the church, thou shalt give heed unto all his [Joseph] words and commandments which he shall give unto you as he receiveth them, walking in all holiness before me; For his word ye shall receive,

---

1. According to the laws of the state of New York, at least thirty people were required to organize a new church, six of whom functioned as official incorporators. The incorporators were Joseph Smith Jr., Oliver Cowdrey, Hyrum Smith, Samuel Smith, David Whitmer, and Peter Whitmer Jr.
2. See section header to Doctrine and Covenants 21.

as if from mine own mouth, in all patience and faith" (D&C 21:4–5; emphasis added).

What would you have thought when you heard this? Would you have had any doubts, any reservations? "This man is young, and clearly like me," you might have said to yourself. "Rough, uneducated, a laborer. A nobody! Why then are these people agreeing to give heed to all of his words and commandments? Does he seriously expect me to consider his words as if they came from God's mouth directly? What makes his words any more valuable than any other person's? And if I accept him, what do I do if I disagree with what he says or the counsel he provides? This feels like a great surrender of my own right to think and act for myself." The audacity of the statements would have inspired some serious reflection. "Certainly, these people are mistaken to give away so much to someone like this."

The hypothetical challenge you would have faced then is the same challenge that those who sustain Joseph Smith's successors face today. Members of The Church of Jesus Christ of Latter-day Saints covenant to "receive the words" of prophets and apostles *as if* from the mouth of the Savior "in all patience and faith" (D&C 21:5). As part of every member's baptismal covenant, individuals freely agree to sustain the President of The Church of Jesus Christ of Latter-day Saints, the First Presidency, and the Quorum of the Twelve Apostles—an obligation that is renewed several times per year at general conference and at stake conferences around the world. Interestingly, the Lord introduced this requirement concurrent with the reorganization of His Church to ensure that the foundation of His Church was firmly established upon His words as given to his servants the prophets (see Ephesians 2:20).

That this requirement was given from the beginning should give us pause. So many aspects of Church culture can be traced to the organization's founding.[3] The Lord is making it clear from the outset that within His Church, the voice to which we should listen to will be His and no other—a voice that will be delivered to His Saints "through His servants the prophets" (Amos 3:7).

---

3. EH Schein, *Organizational Culture and Leadership*, 3rd ed (San Francisco: Jossey Bass, 2004), 225.

For many, fulfilling the covenantal obligation to follow the Lord's servants is increasingly difficult in the modern world. Now, more than any time in history, the sheer number of voices that can be accessed is accelerating through the aid of social media. In addition, any voice can be amplified in the public square, creating information asymmetries between truth and error, the informed and the misinformed. As a result, it is easier than ever for even the most faithful among us to be deceived, just as Jesus prophesied would happen (see Matthew 24:24)—"carried about by every wind of doctrine" (Ephesians 4:14).

The apostolic foundation of the Church of Jesus Christ ensures that members can both overcome the world by faith and find joy in so doing. The collective voice of the First Presidency and Quorum of the Twelve Apostles protects us from forces that pull us away from the covenant path, while providing us the needed perspective to correctly interpret events around us—events that could entice us to adopt alternative voices that would shape our perspectives and influence our bearings in the world. Learning to attune our minds and hearts to the Lord's voice as delivered through His servants requires us to frequently suspend many of our own perceptions and attitudinal preferences. We must wait upon the Lord for His arm to be revealed in His own time and according to His own way. Only when we decide—knowingly decide—to choose the Lord's voice over other enticements can we come to accept His will and receive the assurance that our thoughts, attitudes, and actions are according to His will. Only then can we come to realize that the full intention of the plan of salvation is to bring us happiness, which, as it turns out, is another name for God's plan (see Alma 42:8).

What we choose to be guided by is a consequence of what or who we choose to identify with. The Lord has indicated—in no uncertain terms—that His people are to choose Him as the primary focus of their lives (see Joshua 24:15). Our worship focuses exclusively on Him (see Exodus 20:3).[4] Yet, for many of us, the Lord's declarative remains elusive. The tugs and pulls of the world move us from the

---

4. President Russell M. Nelson has reiterated this idea recently in general conference. See Nelson, "Let God Prevail," October 2020 general conference.

strait[5] and narrow path, little by little, in small increments. Each of us can benefit, then, by discerning information that is both true and aligned with the Lord's voice from that which is not. Furthermore, learning to recognize information that is true and aligned with the Lord's will is essential to correctly assessing the impact of poor information upon our individual identities and enduring well the trials and circumstances of our lives. This book provides the mental framework and tools to enable each of us to follow the Lord's servants more fully and faithfully, because—as the Lord indicated—doing so will require "patience and faith."

---

5. A strait is a narrow neck of water that connects two separate bodies of water, just as the strait and narrow path is a covenant pathway connecting us to God (see 1 Nephi 8 and 2 Nephi 31). A strait path can and does change direction and altitude, which of course makes it challenging and should not surprise those who enter therein. The covenant path is also straight, meaning that it both moves directly toward the intended target of Jesus Christ and is plain and understandable (see 2 Nephi 9:41).

CHAPTER 1

We Are Children of God

Galatians 3:26

Early in the process of the restoration of the gospel, Joseph Smith articulated a difficulty common to all men—particularly members of the Church. He used the idea of a fence as a metaphor to describe the challenge. He said: "The great thing for us to know is to comprehend what God did institute before the foundation of the world, [but] who knows it? It is the constitutional disposition of mankind *to set up stakes and set bounds* to the works and ways of the Almighty."[1] By stakes, Joseph had in mind large posts that stick into the earth and across which lay rails or boards to make a fence.

FENCES

According to the metaphor, the purpose of the fence is to keep out any truth or teaching that contradicts commonly held beliefs or traditions. Additionally, he warned, "I say to all those who are disposed to set up stakes for the Almighty, you will come short of the glory of God. To become a joint heir of the heirship of the Son, one must put away all his false tradition."[2]

To effectively put away false traditions, many of which we cannot currently see, we must identify any of our beliefs that are incorrect and accept all truth. However, in doing so, we are warned against rejecting

---

1. *Teachings of Presidents of the Church: Joseph Smith*, 265.
2. Ibid.

anything which God has revealed through His prophets; His prophet's words are to remain sacrosanct. "I never heard of a man [or woman] being damned for believing too much," said the Prophet, "but they are damned for unbelief."[3] The directive to keep our minds wide open to all sources of truth, while filtering out the thoughts and beliefs which are incorrect—and while accepting the words of living prophets—is both empowering and sobering. It is empowering because it gives each of us liberty of conscience to believe all kinds of things, without being condemned by the Lord, as we sort out true beliefs from false ones. On the other hand, failure to accept even a small portion of that which the Lord has revealed makes all the difference between enlightenment and condemnation—between finding truth or remaining in the dark at noonday.

The Lord's revelations to the prophets provides us with guideposts in our search for truth. His commandments are meant to help us discern truth from error and enable us to accept much more truth than we currently do while laying aside beliefs, attitudes, and mindsets that fence error into our minds. Some stakes can be so deeply dug that they do not come out easily—or at once. Indeed, some of our mental fencing can be more like the Berlin Wall, layered with barbed wire, and watched over by men with guns. To go near some of our fences with the intent to take them down can invite an array of protective and defensive maneuvers. Nevertheless, as was the case with the Berlin Wall, all fences can come down if we can find the right tools for the job. The tool to remove the stakes from our minds that block us from receiving all truth is a mental construct called identity.

IDENTITY

The word "identity" is used in many different contexts. It is an idea or concept that you find at the center of multiple academic and professional disciplines. In simple terms, identity is the mental construct we hold of ourselves, oftentimes unarticulated, which gives us our sense of purpose and belonging.[4] It is developed by the stories

---

3. Ibid, p. 265.
4. P. Burke, *Relationships Among Multiple Identities.* P. O. Burke, ed. (New York: Kluwer Academic Plenum, 2003); J. Simmons and G. McCall, *Identities and*

we tell ourselves,[5] stories based upon a belief that we are either worthy of redemption or are contaminated emotions serving no ultimate purpose.[6] It is the sum total of "qualities, beliefs, personality traits, appearance, and/or expressions that characterize a person or group."[7] A person's identity answers the question, "To whom or to what do I pledge my allegiance?" Depending on the person, the answers to that question can be nuanced and take a variety of forms. Since World War II, much research has been conducted on the importance of identity in influencing behavior. Results across a host of disciplines tell the same story: Our identity influences both *what* we think and *how* we think and, therefore, is highly predictive of a person's behavior.

Identity research has shown the concept to be more complex than one might think. For one thing, identity is multi-faceted, meaning that our identities consist of many dimensions, or sub-identities, that reflect the myriad of ways that we present ourselves to the world. Each facet has associated attitudes, assumptions, beliefs, and behaviors, which, when taken together, form a mental model[8] or pattern that affects what we see around us. In general, the facets of our identities overlap around core beliefs and behaviors that allow us to be seen and experienced by others, with the multitude of identity facets reinforcing one another. However, oftentimes this is not the case, and our identities compete with one another for prominence in our lives. This is especially true when behavioral requirements are in conflict. Consider the teenager whose dancing talent and competitive dance club performance schedule contend with her family vacation schedule and her church's sabbath day worship. Each identity—that of dance team member, family

Interaction: An examination of Human Associations in Everyday Life (New York: Free Press, 1978); B. Verplanken and R. Holland, "Motivated Decision-Making: Effects of Activation and Self-Centrality of Values and Choices and Behavior," *Journal of Personality and Social Psychology*, 2003, 83, 434–47; L. Ackerman, *Identity is Destiny* (Oakland, CA: Berrett-Koehler, 2000).

5. D. McAdams, "The psychology of life stories," *Review of General Psychology 5*, no. 2, 2001, 100–122.

6. D. McAdams, *The redemptive self: Stories Americans Live by, revised and expanded edition* (New York: Oxford University Press, 2013).

7. https://en.wikipedia.org/wiki/Identity_(social_science).

8. P. Senge, *The Fifth Discipline: The Art and Practice of the Learning Organization* (Doubleday, 1990). See Chapter 10: "Mental Models."

member, and religious observer—has its own behavioral and attitudinal requirements. The identity she chooses to follow will be strengthened, while the others will be weakened. Sometimes parents intervene with behavioral compulsion, and through their methods, they unintentionally solidify a facet of their child's identity that they would rather weaken. It is important to note that identities are strengthened in the mind by choice, even if a person cannot act upon them freely.

The concept of diversity relates to the discussion of individual identity. In the term's broadest sense, diversity results from individuals possessing multi-faceted identities. It is from the many facets of our identity that we show up differently to one another and through which our many gifts can be expressed. I believe this variety is one of the great gifts of our Heavenly Father to the world—a gift that challenges us to apply the saving doctrines of the gospel of Jesus Christ and that invites us to be like Him. So many of our challenges in life are a result of us clumsily, and sometimes unwillingly, dealing with the individual diversity that surrounds us. Additionally, diversity can become a separate facet of identity—a facet complete with beliefs and behaviors that compete with the other facets for our attention. In this sense, diversity is not a gift but a type of mental fence that can keep us from enjoying all that God wishes us to enjoy.

Beyond the multi-faceted aspects, our identities are also contextual. This means that depending on our context, certain identities assume an ascendant position relative to their counterparts and the associated behaviors and mindsets are manifest in kind. Some of these contexts were developed in our youth, so when we go home to visit family, for instance, and socialize with those who knew us, say, as a "kid brother," or "comedian," we choose to accommodate such contexts by reverting to a familiar storyline that dictates how we speak and act. We discover these identities over the passage of a few years as we mature and our relationships to our family members change. Other contexts, however, have long traditions and histories associated with them, and we can no longer see how immersed we are in them. Nationality, race, and ethnic or cultural heritage are examples of such facets of identity. These facets are more stable and change less frequently and dramatically, so our relationship to them and our choices about them can be more obscured—that is, until certain beliefs and behaviors are brought into conflict with our other facets of identity. As is the case with our family contexts, we likewise inherit these facets—facets that establish certain facts about us. With that said, such facts need not define how and what we think. We can make choices about the implications of these contexts and change our behavior accordingly.

Sometimes facets of our identity can trap us into relational patterns that are painful or difficult to change because of the strength of contextual cues. Strong family or ethnic cultures, for example, may have normative expectations that are very difficult to abandon because doing so may hurt another and we do not want to cause harm. Or sometimes we simply do not know how to live differently without sacrificing the behavioral and attitudinal expectations of the contextual identity to which we no longer feel drawn. The appeal of contextual facets of identity can weaken or strengthen over time as we gain different life experiences and dealing with the implications of such changes can be very difficult to negotiate with friends and family members with whom we have shared so many memories and history. The reality of contextual change that we experience leads us to consider an additional facet of identity: fluidity.

Our identities are not static. Each is subject to change over time as we gain more experience in different contexts and learn new things. Sometimes information we learn invites us to adopt new facets that compete with the beliefs, attitudes, and behaviors of some of our existing facets of identity. When this happens, we have a choice to decide which facet is more important to us. The changing nature of our identity is very important because it means that we do not have to remain as we are. We can adopt new facets with accompanying beliefs, attitudes, and behaviors and change our identity. It also means that beliefs and behaviors which today are very important to us might not remain so as we gain new experiences and learn new information. We also have the ability to deepen existing facets of identity—to drive mental stakes, as it were, more deeply into the ground through the same processes of learning and doing.

The fluidity of identity helps us pause when adopting assumptions of facets which may not be correct. This is particularly true with socially constructed facets, such as nationality, culture, and race. On its face, that last sentence may seem surprising—even lunatic—but consider that in our lifetimes we have seen the dissolutions of nations and institutions that shaped culture and imbibed meaning into their citizenry. The rapid dissolution of the Soviet Union left millions of people without a nation and suddenly free to identify with a new nationality. For many people around the world, nations—like their attending governments—rise and fall. The Catholic church, an institution rich in tradition and historically prescriptive in normative cultural requirements, no longer carries the same influence among its adherents generally nor in the nations that have long hosted so many of its parishioners. Even race, something that seems so absolute, is being reexamined for its complexity. As it turns out, our terminology and institutions have done much to oversimplify what has always been an intricate and evolving part of each of us. Just browse through some old US census forms to see how the perception and categorization of race has changed in our lifetimes. Or visit a country such as Brazil or Argentina and witness literal melting pots of ethnic traditions, where citizens do not see race as a homogenous characteristic but rather as one ingredient in the alchemy of the individual.

As interesting as the first three facets of identity are—multi-faceted, contextual, and fluid—the last two aspects are perhaps the most significant: the facets of our identities are hierarchical and a function of moral agency. Let us consider the former first.

Facets of identity are hierarchical in that they compete with each other for primacy in our lives. One facet will always win out among all others and become primary to us. It is this facet of identity—our primary facet—that is absolutely essential to understand because the implications of it are so profound. This is because our primary facet is the facet through which all other facets are viewed. It carries with it real demands in thought and action. Our primary facet of identity is not mental accent. Adherents with similar primary facets of identity will reject anyone who is not completely and fully a member in thought and action. Compromise of viewpoints and behaviors will not be an option. It is the primary lens through which we see the world. It shades all of the beliefs, attitudes, and behaviors of our secondary and tertiary facets of identity. In this way, it acts like a type of optical filter (see Figure 1).

Figure 1: Optical Filter

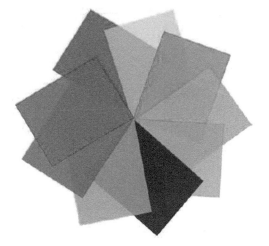

An optical filter is a device that selectively transmits light of different wavelengths, usually implemented as a glass plane or plastic device. Filters of this kind selectively transmit light in a particular range of wavelengths, or colors, while absorbing the remainder. The resulting color we see is determined by the filter in the primary or top position. Our primary identity facet works similarly in relation to the other facets of our identity, in that it colors and selectively shades the other facets. Any truth that passes through is only a particular wavelength and not the complete spectrum. It is a permeable, mental fence that sets the terms for what we see, think, and come to accept as true.

Selecting a facet of identity as primary does not mean it ceases to collaborate with other facets. Rather, it is through our primary facet of identity that we filter incoming information, interpret facts, and determine meaning. Our primary identity affects how and what we think by selecting the wall against which we lean our Ladders of Inference[9] and is comparable to a mental model.[10] We will discuss these concepts in detail in chapter 3.

---

9. Chris Argyris and Donald A. Schon, *Organizational Learning II: Theory, Method, and Practice* (Reading, Mass: Addison-Wesley, 1996). See also chapter 4.
10. Senge, ibid. "New insights, fail to get put into practice because they conflict with deeply held internal images of how the world works, images that limit

Primary identity facets provide us with specific benefits. For example, certain professional facets of identity have been shown to protect individuals from anxiety and despair in the face of uncertainty. Consider a study of airline pilots facing organizational uncertainty during merger and acquisition announcements. The researchers conducting the study, concluded: "Despite their uncertainty and declining attitudes, the pilots continued to like their work and to be committed to it. . . . This is because they adopted a professional or occupational orientation instead of an organizational one."[11]

The pilots accomplished this by "allowing priorities for professional affiliation help them reframe the importance of uncertainty about the employing organization . . . by re-evaluating the organizational ownership as less important than their professional identities—I'm a pilot, and that matters more than the company that employs me." Pilots chose to place their identities as pilots above their identities as employees. Doing so helped them press forward in the face of uncertainty and be less concerned with seeking out information about the merger. Our primary facets of identity can make us resilient in the face of the unknown.

Another reason our primary facet of identity requires our allegiance is that it is the source from where we draw purpose and meaning for our lives. As a result, we choose to give everything we have over to this way of thinking and acting.

And that leads to the final point about identity—the most important point of all—identity is a function of moral agency.

PRIMARY IDENTITY AND MORAL AGENCY

We choose our primary facet of identity, along with every other facet of identity in our lives. We decide which facet will be primary and to which we will give our allegiance. *We decide.* This reality carries

---

us to familiar ways of thinking and acting. . . . Our mental models determine not only how we make sense of the world, but how we take action" (174–75).

11. M. Kramer, D.S. Dougherty, and T. A. Pierce, "Managing Uncertainty during a corporate acquisition: A longitudinal study of communication during an airline acquisition," *Human Communication Research*, 2004, 30 (1), 71–101.

deep implications. It implies that regardless of our genetic, environmental, or spiritual inheritance, we decide which facet of identity will shape how we see the world and from which facet all of our actions will flow. We can determine how many facets of identity we will adopt and determine the contexts in which those identities are exercised. We choose which facets we will strengthen and which we will weaken, and we choose which identity will be primary above all.

This is not to say that we choose the conditions of mortality that are genetically or environmentally inherited. For instance, someone who lives with same gender attraction did not choose to be gay. However, a gay person can and does choose how and to what extent his or her facet of identity as a gay person will interact with his or her other facets. The same is true for other inherited mortal conditions such as race, ethnicity, or physical health conditions. A Samoan man or woman, for example, arrives in mortality in a family with varying emphasis placed on his or her ethnic identity facet, but it is ultimately that person's choice as to what extent those beliefs, attitudes, and behaviors will influence his or her life relative to other competing facets.

It is because of our divine endowment of moral agency that we can avoid setting up mental stakes that block our acceptance of divine truth. And it is because of our moral agency that we correctly identify the influences in our lives that are not aligned with the truth flowing to and through the Lord's living servants the prophets.

Some writers have described the tension between the benefits flowing from our agency and the gospel requirement to be obedient as a paradox,[12] but they acknowledge that it is through such paradoxes that one comes to know the truth.[13] The key is to not let facets of identity that are filled with error or bad assumptions have sufficient sway over our thoughts and actions that we unintentionally reject truth before it can be fully manifest. We can, if we are not careful, be influenced by a primary facet of identity. As a result, we misinterpret certain frustrating conditions, short-change

---

12. T. Givens, *People of Paradox: A History of Mormon Culture* (New York: Oxford University Press, 2007), chapter 1.

13. P. Mason, *Planted: Belief and Belonging in an Age of Doubt* (Salt Lake City: Deseret Book, 2015), 161.

our access to truth, and stymie our spiritual development. We literally fence ourselves into a corner by our own choosing, becoming completely unaware of the limitations we have placed upon ourselves—limitations that keep us from the "fulness of truth" that our Heavenly Father wants us desperately to enjoy.[14] Speaking on the importance of our agency to determine how and what we think, President Russell M. Nelson taught:

> We set our own priorities and determine how we use our energy, time, and means. We decide how we will treat each other. We choose those to whom we will turn for truth and guidance. The voices and pressures of the world are engaging and numerous. But too many voices are deceptive, seductive, and can pull us off the covenant path. To avoid the inevitable heartbreak that follows, I plead with you today to counter the lure of the world by making time for the Lord in our life each and every day.[15]

Getting our primary facet of identity right also helps us as we "press forward" (2 Nephi 31:20) along the covenant path. One of the most uncomfortable details of the Lord's plan for us is that "he will try our patience and faith" (Mosiah 23:21). Our primary facet of identity is essential in helping us not only survive from day to day but "endure well" (D&C 121:8), "endure in faith" (D&C 101:35), and "endure valiantly" (D&C 121:29). Most importantly, our primary facet should direct us to look to the Savior as we endure (see 3 Nephi 15:9). It should help us accept the injunction of President Nelson to "let God prevail in our lives."[16]

The challenge of choosing for ourselves can be daunting. Still, the living prophets beckon us onward. As President Nelson has said, "The question for each of us . . . is the same. Are you willing to let God

---

14. D&C 93:19–20: "I give unto you these sayings that you may understand and know how to worship, and know what you worship, that you may come unto the Father in my name, and in due time receive of his fulness. For if you keep my commandments you shall receive of his fullness and be glorified in me as I am in the Father; therefore, I say unto you, you shall receive grace for grace."
15. Russell M. Nelson, "Make Time for the Lord," *Ensign*, October 2021.
16. Nelson, "Let God Prevail," *Ensign*, October 2020.

prevail in your life? Are you willing to let God be the most important influence in your life? Will you allow His words, His commandments, and His covenants to influence what you do each day? Will you allow His voice to take priority over any other? Are you willing to let whatever He needs you to do take precedence over every other ambition? Are you willing to have your will swallowed up in His?"[17]

The scriptures attest that our ultimate potential can only be found in patterning our life after Jesus Christ. Jesus Christ is the way to eternal life, which is the opportunity to accept all truth and learn and grow eternally. Our Savior's question applies to all of us: "What manner of men ought ye to be? Verily I say unto you, even as I am" (3 Nephi 27:27). The model below (Figure 2) diagrams how the Savior's invitation to become "even as I am" is linked to the choices we make as we determine our identity.

Figure 2: Striving to Become like Jesus

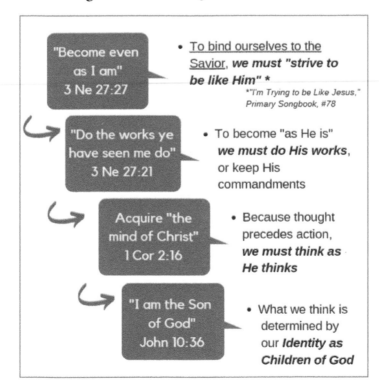

JESUS CHRIST'S IDENTITY AS THE SON OF GOD

Jesus showed us what our primary identity should be. Our Heavenly Father has likewise made this identity central to His plan by emphasizing His Fatherhood and Jesus's divine Sonship. From the time Adam and Eve partook of the forbidden fruit and were cast out of the garden of Eden, the Father has mediated His relationship to us through His Only Begotten Son (see Moses 4:28). On certain occasions when the Father has appeared unto His children on earth, He has deliberately introduced His Only Begotten to us—an important gesture that emphasizes both the importance of Jesus to His plan of salvation as well as His Son's divine identity (see Matthew 3:17; 17:5; 3 Nephi 11:7; and JS—H 1:17).

While in mortality, Jesus made His primary identity the Only Begotten Son of God. When comparing Jesus's life to the five dimensions of identity considered earlier, we see evidence of each in the scriptures. For instance, like each of us, Jesus's identity was multifaceted and contextual, influenced by early life experiences in His family, country of origin, profession, and other facets. Yet, unlike us, Jesus had no issue subjecting these facets to His identity as a child of God. As I wrote in my book, *Renewing your Relationship with Jesus,*

> Despite the efforts of many around Him to define him differently, Jesus was emphatic on His primary identity. Jesus could have chosen to define himself based on formative experiences from his youth (a refugee) or where he was reared (Nazareth). He might have elected to identity with his profession (carpenter) or by his unique abilities to promulgate wine and bread (miracle worker). He could have identified as a misunderstood victim, mischaracterized by others as a sinner, but he did not. No, to Him, what mattered most was his identity as the Only Begotten Son of God (see Matthew 3:17) and Messiah (see John 4:25-26). To Jesus, His identity as the Son of God was chief among all of his other identities (Luke 2:42–49).[18]

---

18. J. Savage, *Renewing Your Relationship with Jesus* (Springville, Utah: Cedar Fort Inc., 2001), 26–30.

It was Jesus's testimony of His relationship to His Father that brought constant danger (see John 5:18). Nevertheless, it was His assurance of this relationship that kept Him laser focused on His Father's works (see John 5:19). It was also this identity that led Him to emulate His Father's works, doing "all things that himself doeth" (John 5:20). Someday we will come to appreciate this verse more than at present.

Jesus's identity was also fluid, changing as He aged and gained more experience. We see examples of such fluidity in His youth as He attended the temple with His family (see Luke 2:42–51). The age of twelve was a critical age when a boy could transition into young adulthood and become a student of the law. Jesus's awareness of such a transition was not lost upon Him as He counseled Mary and Joseph as they searched for Him. "How is it that ye sought me? wist ye not that I must be about my Father's business?" (Luke 2:49), He asked, emphasizing again His identity as God's son. Similarly, the scriptures describe His maturation to adulthood and His willingness to "grow up with his brethren while He "wait[ed] upon the Lord for the time of his ministry" and "serve[ed] under his earthly father," insights that all point toward His willingness to assume the duties and activities of such associations up until the time when they would no longer be required of Him (see JST, Matthew 3:24–26).

Finally, consider the wedding at Cana, when His mother approached Him and asked for His help in securing wine. His public ministry hadn't yet begun. To her, He replied, "Woman, what wilt thou have me to do for thee? that will I do; for mine hour is not yet come" (JST, John 2:4). The Savior's response again indicated that He was willing to participate in everyday, even mundane tasks, such as helping family members throw a successful party. However, once the time arrived for His public ministry to begin, such things would be set aside—prioritized, as it were—to the chores of His child of God identity which remained primary in his life.

Jesus's identity as the Son of God gave Him direction on what to do on a daily basis. Direction flowed to Him as He kept His identity as the Only Begotten Son of God paramount among His hierarchy of identity facets. It was through this identity that all other potential choices were filtered. He said, "For I came down from heaven, not to do mine own will, but the will of him that sent me" (John 6:38). And it was because Jesus aligned Himself first with His Father's will that He gained the assurance of His Father's help when needed. "And he that sent me is with me," He said. "The Father hath not left me alone; for I do always those things that please him" (John 8:29).

Such daily decisions reflect real submission of Jesus's mind and heart to the will of His Father. Of such submission, Abinadi testified:

> And because he dwelleth in flesh he shall be called the Son of God, and having subjected the flesh to the will of the Father, being the Father and the Son. . . . And thus the flesh becoming subject to the Spirit, or the Son to the Father, being one God, suffereth temptation, and yieldeth not to the temptation, but suffereth himself to be mocked, and scourged, and cast out, and disowned by his people. . . . Yea, even so he shall be led, crucified, and slain, the flesh becoming subject even unto death, the will of the Son being swallowed up in the will of the Father. (Mosiah 15:2–7)

As demonstrated by Jesus, the real test is not to give away our facets of identity. The real test is to have them "swallowed up"—each and every moment of each and every day—in something bigger and grander than we, even "swallowed up in the will of the Father."

Significantly, it was upon the grounds of Jesus's identity as the Son of God that Satan challenged Him directly. Prior to Jesus's public ministry, while He was communing with His Father in the wilderness, Satan came tempting him with the words, "If thou be the Son of God" (Matthew 4:3). Of this encounter, Elder James E. Talmage has written, "The Eternal Father had proclaimed Jesus as His Son; the devil tried to make the Son doubt that divine relationship . . . To have yielded would have been to manifest positive doubt of the Father's acknowledgement."[19] Similarly, on the cross and near the end of His mortal ministry, Jesus was once again tormented with the same challenge to His divine identity by "they that passed by" who "reviled him" (Matthew 27:39–40). Once again, Jesus was able—because of

---

19. James E. Talmage, *Jesus the Christ*, 4th edition (Salt Lake City: The Church of Jesus Christ of Latter-day Saints, 1982), 121.

His reliance on His identity as the Son of God—to "suffer temptations but give no heed unto them" (D&C 20:22).

No one had their moral agency more tested than Jesus; yet, even in this final dimension of identity, His choices were so sublimely aligned to His Father's will. It was to the Nephites that Jesus made this awe-inspiring admission of how He exercised his agency during His mortal probation: "And behold, I am the light and the life of the world; and I have drunk out of that bitter cup which the Father hath given me, and have glorified the Father in taking upon me the sins of the world, in the which *I have suffered the will of the Father in all things from the beginning*" (3 Nephi 11:11; emphasis added).

Suffering can mean a person experienced something difficult. It also means that someone allows something to happen to them. When Jesus says that He "suffered the will of the Father in all things from the beginning," He is referencing His decision—His conscious and willing choice—to let His Heavenly Father's will be the primary identity in his life. In this way, He is choosing to endure everything and anything the Father "seeth fit to inflict upon him, even as a child doth submit to his Father" (Mosiah 3:19). This Jesus chose to do, as He testified in our day:

> For behold, I, God, have suffered (chose and experienced) these things for all, that they might not suffer if they would repent; But if they would not repent they must suffer even as I; Which suffering caused myself, even God, the greatest of all, to tremble because of pain, and to bleed at every pore, and to suffer both body and spirit—and would that I might not drink the bitter cup, and shrink—Nevertheless, glory be to the Father, and I partook and finished my preparations unto the children of men. (D&C 19:16-19)

OUR PRIMARY IDENTITY AS CHILDREN OF GOD

As was true in the case of Jesus, the ever-relentless adversary applies similar tactics in his attempts to persuade each of us to reject our child of God identity. Remember the experience of Moses. The Lord had appeared to him to teach him of his divine identity, saying, "I have a work for thee, Moses, my son; and thou art in the similitude of mine Only Begotten" (Moses 1:6). Soon afterward, Satan appeared as well. We read: "Satan came tempting him, saying: Moses, *son of man*, worship me" (Moses 1:12; emphasis added). Moses withstood Satan's attacks by remembering his divine identity as a son of God. Said Moses, "Behold, I am a son of God, in the similitude of his Only Begotten; and where is thy glory, that I should worship thee?" (Moses 1:13).

From that time, and from the beginning of time, prophets of God have taught this to each of us: that we are children of God, His sons and daughters, "created after their likeness and image" (Genesis 1:2–27) and in the similitude of His Only Begotten Son! Of this encounter, Elder Gary E. Stevenson testified: "You are a cherished, beloved child of Heavenly Father. He loves you so perfectly that He sent His Son, Jesus Christ, to atone for you and for me. . . . Remembering this love can help you push back the confusion of the world that tries to weaken your confidence in your divine identity and blind you of your potential."[20]

Latter-day prophets have repeatedly taught we are children of God and that this identity should be foremost in our lives. In "The Family: A Proclamation to the World," the Council of the First Presidency and Quorum of the Twelve Apostles proclaimed, "All human beings— male and female—are created in the image of God. Each is a beloved spirit son or daughter of heavenly parents, and, as such, each has a divine nature and destiny."[21]

Our identity as children of God is so familiar to members of the Church that we take it for granted. We fail to realize the perspective this identity provides us while simultaneously helping us discern truth from error. President Ballard has recently testified:

---

20. Gary E. Stevenson, G., "Deceive Me Not," Oct 2019 general conference. See also B. Taylor, "Am I a Child of God?", October 2021 general conference.
21. "The Family: A Proclamation to the World, The Church of Jesus Christ of Latter-day Saints"; see also, Tad R. Callister, "Our Identity and Destiny," *BYU Speeches*, August 14, 2012.

Jesus wants us to know God is a loving Heavenly Father. Knowing that we are loved by our Heavenly Father will help us know who we are and know that we belong to His great eternal family. . . . Believing that God loves us and that we are His children is comforting and assuring. Because we are the spirit children of God, everyone has a divine origin, nature, and potential. Each of us "is a beloved spirit son or daughter of heavenly parents." This is our identity! This is who we really are! . . . Never forget that you are a child of God, our Eternal Father, now and forever.[22]

President Nelson has emphasized this relationship as essential in helping each of us "let God prevail in our lives." It is essential because it is through the covenants of the gospel that we become "one of God's covenant children, whether by birth or adoption. Each child becomes a full heir to all that God has promised the faithful children of Israel."[23]

In spite of the prophetic emphasis of our true identity as children of God, we are oftentimes easily persuaded to make alternate identities primary in our lives. "The vain things of the world" (Alma 39:14) include "every combination of that worldly quartet of property, pride, prominence, and power,"[24] and continually entice us to choose an alternate identity, one associated with beliefs and behaviors that are comfortable in Babylon. Elder Foster, then a member of the Quorum of Seventy, summarized the challenge well, when he said: "In the past, the world competed for our children's energy and time. Today, it fights for their identity and mind. Many loud and prominent voices are trying to define who our children are and what they should believe...The children of the Church sing a song that teaches them about their real identity: 'I am a child of God.'"[25]

---

22. M. Russell Ballard, "Hope in Christ," April 2021 general conference.
23. Russell M. Nelson, "Let God Prevail," October 2022 general conference.
24. Dallin H. Oaks, "Focus and Priorities," April 2001 general conference.
25. B. Foster, "It's Never too Early and It's Never Too Late," October 2015 general conference.

Re-prioritizing our love of God for the "vain things of the world" is not typically done in dramatic fashion. It is as easy and subtle as changing our mind about a topic, or over time, developing a talent or preference for something. This includes little things like getting healthier (dieting or exercising, for example), becoming more politically active, pursuing racial justice or social equality, or defending our constitutional rights. None of these things are wrong. But when placed at the top of our facets of identity, each carries real consequences. The full allegiance that these facets require limits our ability to receive more truth from God. President Dallin H. Oaks has warned us against choosing alternate identities and of their limiting nature in our pursuit of eternal objectives: "'Where will this lead?' is also important in choosing how we label or think of ourselves. Most important, each of us is a child of God with a potential destiny of eternal life. Every other label, even including occupation, race, physical characteristics, or honors, is temporary or trivial in eternal terms. Don't choose to label yourselves or think of yourselves in terms that put a limit on a goal for which you might strive."[26]

Choosing alternate identities as our primary identity also leads us to invert the two great commandments: loving our neighbor first rather than our Father in Heaven. Regarding the sequence of the two great commandments, Jesus was emphatic about which came first— love of God. The first commandment is the greatest of all because it is the greater, and not equivalent to, the second commandment, though it is "like unto it."[27] If the two were equivalent to one another, then they would perhaps be interchangeable. However, because the second

---

26. Oaks,"Where Will This Lead?", April 2019 general conference. See also "Interview with Elder Dallin H. Oaks and Elder Lance B. Wickman: 'Same-Gender Attraction,'" https://newsroom.churchofjesuschrist.org/article/interview-oaks-wickman-same-gender-attraction.

27. Lynn G. Robbins, "Which Way do you Face?," *Church News*, October 2014. "Trying to please others before pleasing God is inverting the first and second great commandments (see Matthew 22:37–39). It is forgetting which way we face. . . . This peer pressure tries to change a person's attitudes, if not behavior, by making one feel guilty for giving offense. We seek respectful coexistence with those who point fingers, but when this fear of men tempts us to condone sin, it becomes a 'snare' according to the book of Proverbs (see Proverbs 29:25). The snare may be cleverly baited to appeal to our compassionate side to tolerate

commandment is second, it is subservient to and dependent upon the first. As the Savior said, the second commandment and every commandment after hang on the first commandment—but only when the first commandment is to love God (see Matthew 25:35–40).

Our first priority above all else is to place our relationship with our Heavenly Father at the forefront of our lives. No matter how worthy or widely acceptable, no alternate identity will do. Only through our identity as sons and daughters of God can all of the weightier things—things that are truly portable—be secured.[28] The scriptures and the words of living prophets are essential in not only revealing what our primary identity should be but also in tethering us to the strait and narrow path. Without such guidance we are all prone to "walk in our own way."[29] On this point, the scriptural record is clear that "there is no other way" (2 Nephi 31:21; Mosiah 3:17; Alma 38:9; Helaman 5:9).

CHILDREN OF GOD IDENTITY: WHAT IT REQUIRES

As is the case with all identities, each come equipped with beliefs and requisite behaviors; the child of God identity is no different. What are some of the beliefs we must accept in order to place this identity at the forefront of our lives? Below are some of the essentials as contained in the scriptures and taught by the Lord's prophets.

---

or even approve of something that has been by God. For the weak of faith, it can be a major stumbling block."

28. Oaks, "Focus and Priorities," April 2001 general conference. "The ultimate Latter-day Saint priorities are twofold: First, we seek to understand our relationship to God the Eternal Father and His Son, Jesus Christ, and to secure that relationship by obtaining their saving ordinances and by keeping our personal covenants. Second, we seek to understand our relationship to our family members and to secure those relationships by the ordinances of the temple and by keeping the covenants we make in that holy place. These relationships, secured in the way I have explained, provide eternal blessings available in no other way. No combination of science, success, property, pride, prominence, or power can provide these eternal blessings!"

29. Neal A. Maxwell, "God Will Yet Reveal," October 1986 general conference.

- We are children of Heavenly Parents; our spirits are created in their image, male and female (see Genesis 1:26–27; Moses 2:26–27; "The Family: A Proclamation to the World").
- Our gender is eternal, inherent in our premortal, mortal, and postmortal identities (see "The Family: A Proclamation to the World").[30]
- Our Heavenly Father has a plan of salvation that applies to us collectively and individually (see Alma 42:5,8,16; Moses 6:62).
- Our Heavenly Father created this earth as a place to receive physical bodies and test our spirits through the exercise of our moral agency (see Abraham 3:24–26).
- To make the pursuit of truth meaningful, mortal choices had to be made between contesting forces of good and evil. Therefore, an adversary is allowed to tempt us to act contrary to God's plan (see 2 Nephi 2:11–20).
- The purpose of God's plan was to give His children the opportunity to choose eternal life. This could be accomplished only by experience in mortality and, after death, by postmortal growth in the spirit world (see 2 Nephi 2:21–27).
- Our Heavenly Father provided a Savior, His Only Begotten Son, to rescue those who accept and live His gospel. He overcame the effects of sin and death thereby enabling us to become new creatures in Him (see Topical Guide, "Jesus Christ").
- "All mankind may be saved by obedience to the laws and ordinances of [His] Gospel" (Articles of Faith 1:3).
- Eternal family relationships can be attained only through an eternal marriage between a man and a woman (see Doctrine and Covenants 131:1–3).

---

30. See *General Handbook: Serving in The Church of Jesus Christ of Latter-day Saints*, 38.6.21 (2022): "Gender is an essential characteristic of Heavenly Father's plan of happiness. The intended meaning of gender in the family proclamation is biological sex at birth. Some people experience feelings of incongruence between their biological sex and their gender identity. As a result, they may identify as transgender. The Church does not take a position on the causes of people identifying as transgender."

These doctrines are fundamental to adopting the child of God identity. They are simple to understand but stand in stark contrast to many of the competing identities in the world today. As a result, they can be impossible to accept unless a change of identity takes place. For so many among us, unanswered questions and difficult life circumstances make a complete acceptance of such doctrines difficult. Those with other primary identities are still sorting through the doctrines, picking and choosing the ones they like from among those that are incompatible with their identities. They live, as it were, straddling the mental fences they have built, yet they sense that such straddling cannot go on forever. They know that at some future point they must choose: either live within the confines of an alternate identity or accept the child of God identity as primary and live with unanswered questions.

Ironically, living within the fences of an alternate identity may provide more short-term mental comfort. "They have their reward," so to speak—for the short-term (see 3 Nephi 13:2, 5, 16). Given its eternal consequences, however, it is a Pascalian wager that they shouldn't make lightly.[31] The full impact of the beliefs and behaviors they surrendered will be manifest in due time.

The child of God identity enables us to become new creatures in Christ. Just as He adopted the identity fully and progressed from grace to grace (see D&C 93:12–13), so too can we. The Lord revealed to Joseph Smith:

> I give unto you these sayings that you may understand and know how to worship, and know what you worship, that you may come unto the Father in my name, and in due time receive of his fulness. For if you keep my commandments you

---

31. https://en.wikipedia.org/wiki/Pascal%27s_wager.

Pascal's wager is a philosophical argument presented by the seventeenth-century Frenchman Blaise Pascal (1623–1662). It posits that human beings wager with their lives that God either exists or does not. Pascal argues that a rational person should live as though God exists and seek to believe in God. If God does not exist, such a person will have only a finite loss (some pleasures, luxury, and so on), whereas if God does exist, He stands to receive infinite gains (as represented by eternity in heaven) and avoid infinite losses (an eternity in hell).

shall receive of his fulness, and be glorified in me as I am in the Father; therefore, I say unto you, you shall receive grace for grace. (D&C 93:19–20)

Like Jesus, empowered with such an identity, we can avoid setting up any 'stakes' and receive all truth: "John bore record of me, saying: He received a fulness of truth, yea, even all truth" (D&C 93:26).

We receive more truth through the child of God identity than any other because of what it permits us to see. We are not limited by what other facets of identity require us to consider as sin. Instead, we see our own sins for what they are and willingly offer a broken heart and contrite spirit to God to rectify them (see 3 Nephi 9:17, 20, 22). Similarly, our obedience is driven by our vision of things as "they really are and really will be" (Jacob 4:13), as Elder Boyd K. Packer explained:

> We are the sons and daughters of God, willing followers, disciples of the Lord Jesus Christ, and "under this head are [we] made free." (Mosiah 5:8). Those who talk of blind obedience may appear to know many things, but they do not understand the doctrines of the gospel. There is an obedience that comes from a knowledge of the truth that transcends any external form of control. We are not obedient because we are blind, we are obedient because we can see.[32]

Our child of God identity also keeps us from excessive handwringing and worry over things "yet to be revealed" (Articles of Faith 1:9) and those places in history where the trail of sources goes cold. This is because we trust in God's character above all else and His godly characteristics of justice, mercy, and omniscience. We become more like Mormon, who made plates not knowing the reason: "And I do this for a wise purpose; for thus it whispereth me, according to the workings of the Spirit of the Lord which is in me. And now, I do not know all things; but the Lord knoweth all things which are to come;

---

32. Boyd K. Packer, "Agency and Control," April 1983, general conference.

wherefore, he worketh in me to do according to his will" (Words of Mormon 1:7).

Such understanding leads us to trust in prophetic direction, acknowledging that we—like them—do not know all things. Yet God does, and that is why we trust Him. We really do believe that God has made "ample provision"[33] for all things to be made right, according to his "own time, and in his own way, and according to his own will" (D&C 88:68). We do not, for example, look ashamedly upon Jesus because of His unwillingness to share His gospel among the Gentiles before the Father willed it, instead confining it to the "lost sheep of the House of Israel" (Matthew 15:24). All things have their time and season in God's plan. Therefore, "the disciple [of Jesus] must be in a posture of constant anticipation," as Elder Maxwell has explained, "yet he can have the serenity and security of knowing."[34]

We do not adopt the posture of alternate identities that demand reparations for injustices. Rather, we are willing to "keep all [such] things and ponder them in [our] hearts" (Luke 2:19) until God sees fit to reveal more to us. We are, like Alma, "content with the things allotted unto us," (Alma 29:3–4), which include our circumstances, our limitations, and our circles of influence. We recognize these things as divinely designed equipment, each one fitting our backs or shoulders precisely constructed to protect and enable us to fight real battles in the here and now, and representative of who we were before, in a now forgotten, pre-mortal life. We know and trust that God will not place anything in our path beyond our ability to overcome with His help.

Similarly, the child of God identity changes our thoughts and invites us to think as the Savior thinks. This is because our child of God identity is influenced more completely by the Holy Ghost. Our thinking then is not limited by the creeds and philosophies of our other identities—identities that are most likely aligned with our immediate needs of the flesh and the fleeting feelings that accompany them. With child of God as our identity, we "have the mind of Christ" (1

---

33. *Teachings of Presidents of the Church—Joseph Smith*, "Chapter 35: Redemption for the Dead" (Salt Lake City: The Church of Jesus Christ of Latter-day Saints, 2007), 407.

34. Maxwell, *Things as They Really Are* (Salt Lake City, 1989), 40.

Corinthians 2:16). Our thoughts are near to, instead of far from, the "thoughts and intents of [the Lord's] heart" (Mosiah 5:13).

Finally, the child of God identity helps us let go of lesser things—like Jesus (see 3 Nephi 11:11)—and submit ourselves fully and completely to His will. Submitting ourselves in this way is the one unique offering we make to God. We may mistakenly conclude that to choose the child of God identity we are somehow surrendering our individuality. Yet in reality, all we really are giving away is a limiting view of self. Elder Maxwell explained:

> What we are really worried about, of course, is not giving up self, but selfish things—like our roles, our time, our preeminence, and our possessions. No wonder we are instructed by the Savior to lose ourselves (see Luke 9:24). He is only asking us to lose the old self in order to find the new self. It is not a question of one's losing identity but of finding his true identity! Ironically, so many people already lose themselves anyway in their consuming hobbies and preoccupations but with far, far lesser things.[35]

Granted, this type of submission is not easy. But ultimately it is the only way, the only identity that enables us to become like a child, reborn and remade, laying aside the natural man in the process of time: "For the natural man is an enemy to God, and has been from the fall of Adam, and will be, forever and ever, unless he yields to the enticings of the Holy Spirit, and putteth off the natural man and becometh a saint through the atonement of Christ the Lord, and *becometh as a child*" (Mosiah 3:19 emphasis added).

RECOGNIZING COMPETING IDENTITIES

The discussion of identity invites two important questions for consideration: How can I know which facets of identity are operating in my life? Which is primary among them?

---

35. Maxwell, "Swallowed up in the Will of the Father," *Ensign*, October 1995.

We can identify the many facets of our identity and then choose which facet will be our primary identity by first discovering more about the facets we have already chosen. This is done by reflecting and answering a few questions about ourselves. Performing this personal inventory of ourselves can be extremely rewarding. It gives us an opportunity to acknowledge truths currently available to us that have perhaps been obscured by long held assumptions and beliefs of competing facets of our identity. We can assess which facets are still valid and which have run their course, and then reconfigure their influence accordingly. To help conduct your own self-assessment, I have provided a worksheet in appendix A titled "Discovering Your Primary Identity Worksheet."

Before assessing our own identity, practice how to recognize the facets of identity in others can be helpful. Consider someone you know, for instance—someone who has decided to no longer worship actively but still believes certain aspects of the gospel to be true and valuable. The construct of identity can provide an effective lens to better understand this person. The following example from the scriptures is useful as we attempt to identify some of the ways competing facets of identity are manifest. Additionally, one could benefit by applying a similar review of other personalities from the scriptures.

PETER, SON OF JONAS

Simon Peter saith unto them, I go a fishing. They say unto him, we also go with thee. They went forth, and entered into a ship immediately; and that night they caught nothing.

But when the morning was now come, Jesus stood on the shore: but the disciples knew not that it was Jesus.

Then Jesus saith unto them, Children, have ye any meat? They answered him, No.

And he said unto them, Cast the net on the right side of the ship, and ye shall find. They cast therefore, and now they were not able to draw it for the multitude of fishes.

Therefore that disciple whom Jesus loved saith unto Peter, It is the Lord.

Now when Simon Peter heard that it was the Lord, he girt his fisher's coat unto him, (for he was naked,) and did cast himself into the sea. . . .

As soon then as they were come to land, they saw a fire of coals there, and fish laid thereon, and bread...

Jesus saith unto them, Come and dine. And none of the disciples durst ask him, Who art thou? Knowing that it was the Lord.

So when they had dined, Jesus saith to Simon Peter, Simon, Son of Jonas, lovest thou me more than these? He saith unto him, Yea, Lord; thou knowest that I love thee. He saith unto him, Feed my lambs.

He saith to him again the second time, Simon, son of Jonas, lovest thou me? He saith unto him, Yea, Lord; thou knowest that I love thee. He saith unto him, Feed my sheep.

He saith unto him the third time, Simon, son of Jonas, lovest thou me? Peter was grieved because he said unto him the third time, Lovest thou me? And he said unto him, Lord thou knowest all things; thou knowest that I love thee. Jesus saith unto him, Feed my sheep. (John 21:3–7, 9, 15–17)

Identity Questions

1. What facets of Peter's identity are evident in this encounter with Jesus?
2. What impact did context have on his primary identity?
3. In spite of what Peter thought of himself, which facet of his identity was primary?
4. How did Jesus invite Peter to choose to reorder the facets of his identity? Hint: Jesus repeatedly emphasized a relationship of Peter's.

Placing our primary identity as a child of God will change everything: It will widen our perspective, increase our faith and trust in God's omniscience, focus our attention on truths that matter most, and fill us with motivations to obey living prophets when faced with incomplete information. Rather than getting hung up on policies or practices of the past which God revealed and prophets faithfully communicated and obeyed, we can trust God—even when we don't fully comprehend—and see His purposes unfold in a myriad of ways as He performs His work, "moving in his majesty and power" (D&C 88:46–48).

Given our limited understanding, a few "big rock" issues are admittedly hard to navigate and make sense of: the need for plural marriage; the abrupt termination and subsequent ban of priesthood privileges from Black members; the limiting of priesthood ordination to worthy males; and the post-resurrection propensities of gay members of the Church. We simply do not know the answers to these questions. Meanwhile, creating reasons for these doctrines or policies, or attempting to justify them based on the belief that the Lord will make all things right—as the scriptures attest He will—has had the opposite effect over time of causing more harm, especially among members with primary identities oriented toward one or more of those issues.

For most of the "big rock" issues, there is a long history of Church leadership—namely prophets—providing explanations only flimsily supported by the scriptures. This has led modern prophets and apostles to assume individual responsibility for their personal writings. Collectively, they have tried to be much more forthright regarding what is known from what isn't.[36] Because of this, the question of prophetic infallibility has been called into question.

Many modern writers—both within and outside of the Church—feel a need to appease the critics with a modern-day attempt to move a camel through the eye of the needle, arguing that prophets are human and make mistakes like all of the rest of us; therefore, we should extend grace to their weakness and errors as we do for all men. This is undoubtedly true. No prophet of the Lord—ancient or modern—has ever proclaimed otherwise. There is a difference between what they reveal as prophets—what the Church then sustains as doctrine and revelations from the Lord—and their mistakes they make as mortals. The former we must accept in "patience and faith" and sustain with

---

36. See "Elder Jeffrey R. Holland Interview" with PBS, https://www.pbs.org/mormons/interviews/holland.html.

our whole hearts and without apology, while the latter we are not required to believe at all.

The child of God identity provides us the greatest amount of latitude to believe anything we want to believe that the Lord hasn't confirmed as true through His prophets. It allows us to believe and sustain the revelation, even in the face of incomplete information, and reject completely any of the reasons given for it, regardless of the source. It allows us to fully sustain and trust prophetic leadership without second-guessing our leaders. The Lord does not indicate anywhere in the scriptures that we are to become skilled at discerning what prophetic counsel is true and should be followed from what is not true and can be ignored. If that was the way He wanted it, there would be no rational justification for having prophets at all. Instead, He has repeatedly made clear that we are "to accept their words as if by my own mouth, in all patience and faith" (D&C 21:5), and that He makes no apologies for what He reveals through His servants, in spite of their weakness: "What I the Lord have spoken, I have spoken, and I excuse not myself; and though the heavens and the earth pass away, my word shall not pass away, but shall all be fulfilled, whether by mine own voice or by the voice of my servants, it is the same" (D&C 1:38).

The child of God identity is essential if we are to ultimately consecrate all that we have. If we are not His children first, we can only give leftovers. And if not His children, then whose children are we? Obviously, someone of far lesser and limited love and who cannot fill us with every needful thing.

CHAPTER 2

"Laying Hold" on Good Information

Helaman 3:29

In His infinite wisdom, the Lord revealed His definition of truth early in the process of restoring all things. To the Prophet Joseph Smith, He said: "Truth is knowledge of things as they are, as they were, and as they are to come" (D&C 93:24). From this definition we can draw at least a few conclusions. First, truth is not relative but absolute, representing things that "are, were, and are to come." Second, it is verifiable to multiple observers and can be tested longitudinally in the past, present, and future. Third, because it exists past, present, and future, truth is situated such that men and women can believe in it first and come to know it second. Belief precedes knowing something is true.[1]

For example, Jesus taught skeptical leaders of His day, "If any man will do his [God's] will he shall know of the doctrine, whether it be of God, or whether I speak of myself" (John 17:7). The implication here is that the doctrines of the gospel—His gospel—are true because anyone can test them by believing in them first and then acting on them and receiving knowledge that they are true. Obeying the doctrines of the gospel carry their own witness that they are true.

This definition of truth is becoming increasingly important in a world that is undergoing a transformation of sorts, where a person's

---

1. Plato offered three requirements for knowledge: 1) justification, 2) belief, and 3) truth.

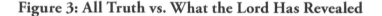

beliefs—beliefs that are subjective and can be born from false conclusions and assumptions from the world around him or her—are now conveniently marketed as "my truth." This subtle shift attempts to make truth not an absolute reality that can be tested and proved, but a relative notion that can be alternatively defined by the bearer as circumstances require. This shift moves us away from traditional philosophical notions of truth—let alone scriptural—that have always defined truth as something "in accordance with facts or reality."[2] Increasingly, it seems that neither element is required for something to be true.

Another important aspect of truth is that it is possessed by God in its fulness, where we mortals only possess it in part (see D&C 93:26-28). Truth is an element which constitutes the glory of God (see D&C 93:36) to which we aspire as we keep his commandments. Because God possesses truth in its fulness, we are well served to remember the portion of it He has revealed to us. The graphic below illustrates this idea (Figure 3).

Figure 3: All Truth vs. What the Lord Has Revealed

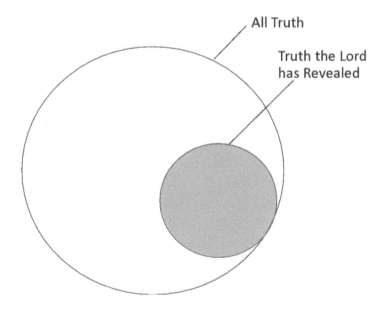

---

2. See *Stanford Encyclopedia of Philosophy*, "Truth," plato.stanford.edu.

The Lord has only revealed a portion—how large or small the portion we do not know. We know it is merely a portion, however, because we likewise believe "He will yet reveal many great and important things pertaining to the kingdom of God (Articles of Faith 1:9).

The fact that it is only a portion implies that there is more to learn for all of us. In several places in the scriptures, the Lord has indicated that what He has revealed, though only a part, is more than enough for us to grapple with.

Related to what is actually true, and the portion that has been revealed, are those aspects of truth that we merely believe and those which we purport to know. I do not think that we give enough consideration—at least I don't—to differentiating between things that we know to be true and things we believe to be true. So many of our actions are based upon belief rather than knowledge—as we will discuss later on—and only in connection to the portion of truth that has been revealed to us from the Lord. Figure 4 shows how belief and truth interact within the revealed portion of truth. Of course, the relative size of the circles in the figure are meant to be relationally representative and not exact dimensions.

Figure 4: What We Know vs. What We Believe

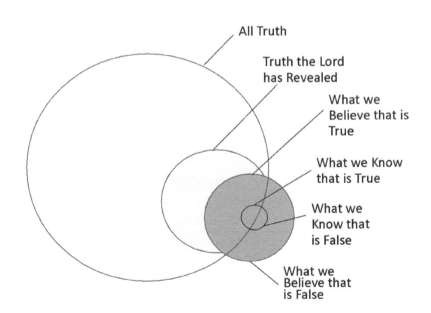

Working from the center of the diagram outward, here are a few observations about Figure 4 that I consider relevant to our discussion of truth:

1. From what the Lord has revealed, we believe much more to be true than what we actually know to be true.
2. What we believe consists of things that are true (revealed by the Lord) and things that are false (not aligned with what the Lord has revealed).
3. Some portion of what we believe and have come to know is true (aligned with what the Lord has revealed).
4. Some portion of what we believe and have come to know is not aligned with what the Lord has revealed, and consequently it is false.

Recall that knowing something is true requires testing it through belief and action. And yet, since life requires time and experience to experiment upon truths in order to know them, we—for a variety of reasons—end up believing most things well before we come to know them. The result is we believe so much more than we know, and so it becomes necessary at this point to examine a few observations concerning the Lord's mercy and grace.

Members of the Church covenant to sustain all of God's revelations, no matter their conclusions or implications, as they are revealed from heaven. We are required to believe "all that God has revealed, all that he does now reveal, and all that he will yet reveal" and nothing more. However, this does not mean that we all know the truth of each revelation immediately or simultaneous to hearing them. The Lord has provided "ample provision" for us to learn and grow in a timeline best suited for our development. Mercifully, He does not condemn us for not knowing something. In short, we are not condemned for believing something that is not true, nor are we condemned for coming to know something that is false—at least not yet. He has provided us the space to come to know what is true, in His timing and according to His own will, when we can finally cast aside every sin and false notion which besets us.

The Lord does care immensely about a condition called unbelief, a condition in which one rejects revealed truth either knowingly or unknowingly. It is the active dilution of light and truth through disobedience and through poor modelling (see D&C 93:39). It is a condition that can be normatively passed on through the "tradition of the fathers" (D&C 3:18), reflecting their own cultural or familial beliefs and behaviors and resulting in a disbelief in the gospel of Christ (see D&C 74:4, 6). This sort of knowing unbelief is actively transmitted by parents to children within the family and happens when active members leave the Church and pull their posterity with them. In time, the rising generation know nothing of God nor His commandments. Or, as is often the case, they inherit the prejudice of their parents toward the Church, its members, or its doctrines.

The Lord has indicated that the effects of knowing unbelief transmitted by parents to their posterity mercifully subside over the course of a few generations. Apparently, it is difficult to maintain proactive instigation of knowing unbelief once the instigators have died. However, just because the carriers of rebellion have passed away, the effects of their crusade against God and His Church still remain, resulting in a condition of unknowing unbelief, or ignorance. People who live in a state of ignorance live in an environmental condition where believing the gospel is constrained due to inherited bias from proceeding generations. The Lord is merciful to ignorance and has a plan to ensure that all ignorance is remedied. He has, by design, arranged things so that His work will not be ultimately frustrated.

For instance, in the Book of Mormon we read of the descendants of Laman and Lemuel who no longer had a problem with the gospel, but—in a state of ignorance—had a continual belief of hatred toward Nephi because of their incomplete view of historical facts:

> They were a wild, and ferocious, and a blood-thirsty people, believing in the tradition of their fathers, which is this— Believing that they were driven out of the land of Jerusalem because of the iniquities of their fathers, and that they were wronged in the wilderness by their brethren, and they were also wronged while crossing the sea; And again, that they were wronged while in the land of their first inheritance, after they had crossed the sea. . . . And again, they were wroth with him when they had arrived in the promised land, because they said

that he had taken the ruling of the people out of their hands; and they sought to kill him. And again, they were wroth with him because he departed into the wilderness . . . and took the records which were engraven on the plates of brass, for they said that he robbed them. And thus they have taught their children that they should hate them, and that they should murder them, and that they should rob and plunder them, and do all they could to destroy them; therefore they have an eternal hatred towards the children of Nephi. (Mosiah 10:12–13, 15–17)

Unbelief is also a condition of the mind and heart. This kind of unbelief results in a darkening of the mind when members "treat lightly" what the Lord has revealed as true (D&C 84:54–55, 76). We treat truth lightly when we dismiss, ignore, or pass over without consideration important doctrines that the Lord has revealed. Such disregard of truth is a source of pain and sorrow to the Lord and to His prophets, as Nephi lamented:

For the things which some men esteem to be of great worth, both to the body and soul, others set at naught and trample under their feet. Yea, even the very God of Israel do men trample under their feet; I say, trample under their feet but I would speak in other words—they set him at naught, and hearken not to the voice of his counsels. (1 Nephi 19:7)

Hearkening not to the voice of the Lord, the God of Israel, is something only done by humans—and oh how often do we do it!

In addition to the darkening of the mind, the heart is also affected by unbelief, primarily through hardening. What is intended to be a pliable and tender muscle becomes stony, repelling not only the Lord's words but also His loving kindness. Hardened hearts make it impossible for members to do the works of Jesus because they cannot feel His Spirit, let alone respond to it. They literally become "past feeling, so that they cannot feel his words" when spoken. This is what happened to Laman and Lemuel (see 1 Nephi 17:45–46). In our own case, such arterial hardening cannot be softened without sincere repentance (see

D&C 58:15), which of course the Lord mercifully and continually extends to each of us (see D&C 38:14).

HOW WE KNOW WHAT WE KNOW

When it comes to verifying truth, philosophers and social scientists have provided several useful tools. One set of tools helps us classify the many kinds of arguments that transmit information and help establish truth. These arguments arm the messages with a kind of validity that makes the words compelling. Though the tools can be applied in a variety of identities, some of these tools are most often tethered to particular facets of identity. In extreme cases, some individuals' use of a single tool is perceived to be of such importance as to establish the identity. With that said, these tools are not antithetical to the child of God identity. In fact, so long as the individual understands the strengths and limitations of the tools, they can help the child of God identity flourish in the face of uncertainty.

THE TOOLS OF KNOWING

There are nine tools of knowing.[3] Each has its own strengths and limitations and is useful in its own way. They include: 1) authoritarianism, 2) rationalism, 3) empiricism, 4) statistical empiricism, 5) pragmatism, 6) skepticism, 7) conscience, 8) personal revelation, and 9) social knowledge. Let's carefully examine each one.

When we know something through authoritarianism, the information has come to us from a person whom we trust to be an authority. So much of what we believe about ourselves and our world we learned through this channel. Social media has accelerated this form of knowing because the requirement of foundational trust is present when we accept others into our social networks. As it turns out, all other tools of knowing are dependant upon authoritarian methods, to a degree, some more than others. The figure below (Figure 5) summarizes the strength and weakness of authoritarianism.

---

3. C. Riddle, *Think Independently* (Chauncey C. Riddle, 2009). This section relies heavily on Professor Riddle's work.

Figure 5: Summary of Authoritarianism

Authoritarianism	Strengths/Weaknesses	Observations
Knowing through communication with other humans. Knowing is predicated on effective and trustworthy communication.	**Strengths** Fastest way to find something out. **Weaknesses** Expertise is required to verify whether information is correct.	Much foundational knowledge is based on our trust in others—name, place and time of birth, parentage, date, time, residence, language, presiding officials, approved medications, laws of the land, and so on.

To understand authoritarianism better, we should keep in mind that an authority does not know everything equally. Learning to recognize that not all of an authority's knowledge is equally authoritative can help us filter less valuable information from valuable. For instance, each of us is an authority on our own thoughts, feelings, and desires, but we are not an authority on the thoughts, feelings, or desires, of another.[4] A physician, for example, may know much about her own thoughts and feelings, but she might know considerably less about the future physical world. Similarly, a president may know extensively about his policy proposals as they are written down or recorded. But he knows considerably less when he is describing how those policies might have affected the world in the past, or how they might affect the future. This is not to say that we cannot forecast the impact of future events based on past experience, merely that there are limitations to what anyone can definitively assert, apart from their own mind, heart, and experience. With that in mind, the continuum of knowing might look something like this:

---

4. This is the foundation for the assertion of "my truth," mentioned earlier. However, just because a person knows something about how they feel or what they think does not make it true, and authoritarianism does not grant this permission either.

Figure 6: What an Expert Can Know Best to What They Can Know Least[5]

Disclosure of a person's thoughts & feelings	Instructions given by a person to do something they have done	Description of the physical world (Here & Now)	Description of the past physical world	Description of the future physical world	Hypotheses of the physical world, past, present, & future

Know Best   **Know Least**

Because no human can know everything about everything, and because we are dependant on the opinions of others to know things that we either do not have the time, interest, or capacity to know for ourselves firsthand, we need methods to evaluate an authority's testimony. These methods are five-fold: 1) compare the testimonies of many persons to the original source; 2) compare the testimonies of others to our own experience; 3) assess the alignment of the testimony with our own beliefs; 4) spend the necessary time exploring to experience the testimony for ourselves; and 5) receive an attestation from the Holy Ghost. It is important to note that only the child of God identity can accommodate all five of these methods. No other identity is capable of wielding the tools of knowing nor of applying the five methods. That is because much of the beliefs associated with competing identities are based on premises that are incorrect—which leads us to a consideration of our second tool of knowing: rationalism.

Rationalism is confirming an idea based on previously held beliefs. To draw good conclusions from rationalism, our underlying beliefs or assumptions must first be correct.[6] We are more likely to draw good conclusions if we begin to form their premises from a point of reference that is true. However, knowing that our beginning point of reference is true is the challenge, since original

---

5. Ibid., 7–9.
6. Ibid., 10–11. Basic forms of rationalism include deduction, drawing a necessary conclusion from given premises based on the rules of inference; induction, deriving a probable conclusion based on information from a sample of evidence from a larger population; and adduction, creating premises from which a given conclusion may be deduced.

points of reference, or axioms, cannot be known through rationalist means; they always start out as an idea or an article of faith. Ironically, all people, religious or not, set their foundations upon articles of faith—faith born from an identity that they have made primary. Knowing this, the believer is fortified in two ways. First, the believer can find comfort in knowing that he or she is not alone in exercising faith in something; and second, when believers understand what articles of faith accompany certain identities, they can apply rational and empirical methods to better evaluate their basis for belief. In so doing, the believer can gain greater clarity for the basis of their belief.

A person is a rationalist if he or she believes that all truth can be made rational or drawn from correct premises. This is an example of what was mentioned at the outset, where a tool of knowing—rationalism—is of such importance to a person that it comes to define him or her.[7]

Rationalism is useful to the child of God identity. In fact, it may be that the child of God identity is the identity most suited to fully utilize the tool of rationalism. This is because it is the child of God identity that provides the correct premises from which to draw conclusions—the truth of "things as they really are, and really will be" (Jacob 4:13). The biggest challenge facing those who embrace the child of God identity occurs when false premises are believed by a majority of people. To introduce premises that contradict what most of society believes invites persecution, which has always been an effective way of persuading members of the Church from the strait and narrow path (see 1 Nephi 8:25–28).

---

7. In my estimation, many great thinkers in western civilization may have chosen to identify themselves this way: Plato, Socrates, and Descartes, to name a few.

Figure 7: Summary of Rationalism

Rationalism	Strengths/Weaknesses	Examples
Certifying an idea because it is deduced from or based on premises that we already believe	**Strengths** If you know you have good premises, then your conclusions are likely sound. **Weaknesses** Challenge to draw good premises/conclusions without correct axioms.	Nearly all theories that we are taught are examples of rationalism. For example, theory of evolution, relativity, human-caused global warming, creationism, intelligent design, human development, social justice, creative destruction, inflation, and so on.

Where rationalism requires the mind to certify information through reason, empiricism requires the rest of the body via the use of one's physical senses and emphasizes personal experience as a way of knowing.[8] Empiricism brings tangible proof into the fray as a necessary requirement—physical evidence that can be seen, held, analyzed, and submitted to testing. It is a fundamental requirement of the scientific method. One famous historical example is Galileo, whose use of the telescope provided visible evidence of the heliocentric nature of our solar system.

The scriptures are replete with examples where the Lord gives evidence that men and women perceive through the use of their physical senses. Usually this is done to provide the necessary perspective that His children need to comprehend something incomprehensible.

Some examples include:

- To Mary after the resurrection of Jesus
- To the man born blind who had his sight restored
- The golden plates of the Book of Mormon

So also was the case with Moses prior to his call to deliver Israel, where the Lord opened his eyes and he "beheld the world and the ends thereof, and all the children of men, which are, and which were created; of the same he greatly marveled and wondered." Of his encounter,

---

8. Famous empiricists include Francis Bacon, John Locke, and Thomas Hobbes.

Moses testified, "Now I know that man is nothing, which thing I never had supposed" (Moses 1:8, 10).

Some things, however, we cannot know through our senses—at least not without help from the Lord. For instance, some things are simply too big for us to comprehend, such as the Earth's size relative to the sun or the sun's position within the Milky Way. Similarly, really small things or things that are far away challenge our senses to detect them. Then there are events that occur distantly that cause outcomes that we experience, such as an earthquake in the South Pacific, for example, miles below the ocean's surface that then produces a tsunami in the Philippines that later raises the prices of mangoes at the local Costcos.

Empiricism also has its limitations in knowing spiritual things. Spiritual knowledge is indeed felt with our physical senses. But the force or power that causes these feelings cannot be observed by someone standing nearby; this other person cannot see, touch, smell, or use any of the other senses to confirm that these feelings are taking place. He or she must depend on the personal witness or disclosure of the person it happened to. Perhaps this is one reason that fast and testimony meeting is so vital to our spiritual development. Without it, we would be limited to our own spiritual experiences without hearing the testimonies of others.

Our senses also limit what we can understand as we observe and experience certain phenomenas. For instance, a person with limited experience and knowledge of auto mechanics does not see, feel, or smell the same things as someone who does have that knowledge. The more we know or the more experience we have with something, the greater our ability to report about it. Unfortunately, our tendency is to see less than what is possible to observe at any moment in time. Our minds tend to notice whatever is most familiar to us, not necessarily what is actually present. This is because what we see is largely determined by what we believe (we will say more about this later). In addition, what we observe and report is influenced heavily by our feelings and our motivations. For instance, the driver who cuts you off can quickly become an enemy filled with evil motives, especially if you are running late for an appointment. The same episode, however, can be interpreted and reported very differently if we are on our way home after a successful day at work.

Finally, when we are experiencing something for the first time, our words as well as our senses fail us. The only way to experience the event then is by analogy—in terms and descriptions we are already familiar with. The scriptures are full of prophets having this type of experience. They see or hear something in vision, something prophetic or futuristic, but can only describe the experience in terms they already know—with descriptions of animals they have already seen, places they have already visited, events that have already taken place, and so forth. This is one reason books like Isaiah or Revelation can be so challenging.

Figure 8: Summary of Empiricism

Empiricism	Strengths/Weaknesses	Examples
The personal use of the physical senses to verify ideas.	**Strengths** Excellent way to verify the truth of assertions for things that are observable. **Weaknesses** 1) Dependant upon pre-existing thoughts or ideas in our minds to comprehend what our senses are telling us. 2) Many important things cannot be known through our senses.	"It was a man, with a gun!" "It looked like a bird, floating in the sky with a long string tied to it." "You are looking for bubbles at the surface." "It started to make a rattling sound, and then I heard a popping sound." Concepts such as love, faith, and mercy are non-sensory.

An increasingly common phenomenon in our modern world is the use of statistics to demonstrate unique relationships between different bodies of information. The goal is to prove that the relationships and correlations aren't just random but that they are predictable and have shared meaning. This method for knowing is called statistical empiricism.

Statistical empiricism is an excellent tool for determining relationships of seemingly disparate pieces of information. However, one must be cautious not to assume correlated information is causal and make faulty conclusions. For instance, ice cream consumption and outside temperature are highly correlated. When it gets hotter, more ice cream is consumed. But it is not ice cream that causes an increase in air temperature. As you can see, using statistical empiricism we could demonstrate correlations to support an endless array of conclusions—conclusions that may or may not be true.

With the accelerated expansion of scientific inquiry, it is becoming more and more difficult to verify the methods used to establish correlations and draw conclusions on a host of topics. The more complex and focused the topic, the more difficult it is to validate the methods used to establish correlations. Thus, we are left to authoritarianism to know what to think or feel—authorities who fashion intriguing empirical arguments.

Figure 9: Summary of Statistical Empiricism

Statistical Empiricism	Strengths/Weaknesses	Examples
Certifying ideas on the basis of correlation between one or more sets of data.	**Strengths** 1) Excellent way to determine correlations. **Weaknesses** 1) Correlations may be coincidence and 2) Possible to make premature conclusions.	"Research has shown the vaccine to be 67 percent effective against the virus." "Exit polls show that 82 percent of voters who support the war effort are from red states."

Though most of us know what we know through multiple tools of knowing, some people do not want to be bothered with statistics or empirical approaches to knowing. Instead, they employ a tool of knowing called pragmatism. Pragmatism, like empiricism, emphasizes knowing through experience but doesn't require proof beyond what is sufficient for the observer. The "proof is in the pudding," as it were.

This way of knowing is described by Alma in his famous discourse on faith, in Alma 32 in the Book of Mormon. Here, Alma likens the word of God to a seed and encourages the Zoramites to "give place" for the word of God, "that it may be planted in your heart," and "if it be a true seed, or a good seed, if ye do not cast it out by your unbelief . . . behold, it will begin to swell within your breast; and when you feel these swelling motions, ye will begin to say within yourselves—it must needs be that this is a good seed . . . for it beginneth to enlarge my soul; yea, it beginneth to enlighten my understanding, yea, it beginneth to be delicious to me" (Alma 32:28). Many members remain active in the Church because of the benefits it provides to their families, or perhaps to their physical health through obeying the Word of Wisdom. They reason, "I may not have a testimony of certain beliefs but it hasn't done me any harm to live this way." This is an example of pragmatism in action.

Other examples exist, of course, of the tool of pragmatism: people who shop at Walmart, leaders who follow certain protocols, athletes who adhere to specific pre-game rituals, and on and on. If it works, why change?

As with the other tools, pragmatism has its own limitations. Sometimes, what we see as the benefits for thinking or behaving in a certain way are not as related as we hope. We make correlations in our mind that are simply coincidence. To make matters worse, some of the reasons we provide for why something works for us may have unintended consequences beyond our ability to anticipate. Remember when smoking was not only believed to be cool but carried no side effects? Or wearing a seat belt was optional? Or any other number of dangerous activities that over time have been demonstrated to carry more risk and severe side effects. This shows up too in our relationships. Most parents can identify an approach used with their children that over time created mental, physical, or psychological side effects years later. So while pragmatism carries obvious benefits, it also requires us to employ other tools of knowing to ensure that we are not becoming our own worst enemy.

Figure 10: Summary of Pragmatism

Pragmatism	Strengths/Weaknesses	Examples
Accepting an idea as true because it works for you.	**Strengths:** Can be used when there is no other access to the truth or falsity of an idea. **Weaknesses:** 1) Correlations may be flawed. 2) Short-term benefits may have long-term negative consequences.	**Trying new or non-traditional therapies.** **Use of products that lead to addiction.** **Concern over appearance or developing talents that lead to narcissistic tendencies, such as an eating disorder.**

Where the prior tools of knowledge rest upon the assumption that truth can be known, there also exists a cautionary tool for knowing called skepticism. In its extreme forms, skepticism asserts that nothing can be known for certain, and therefore the prudent course is to exercise caution against all claims of knowledge. In its more moderate form, skepticism allows for knowing things that can be scientifically tested or backed up by evidence.

Some individuals choose to apply skepticism in a targeted fashion to the realms of religion and philosophy, but not generally. For these individuals, this approach is acceptable because the arenas of religion and philosophy tend to have less empirical evidence and skepticism lends itself well to areas where empirical evidence is lacking. However, it is ironic that even though skepticism is not compelled to accept empirical evidence, its adherents are likely to make an appeal to science as justification for their beliefs nonetheless—as if empiricism were the sole property of this tool of knowing.

The advantage of skepticism is that it prevents one from adopting incorrect beliefs. It also allows a person to compare new information to the beliefs he or she knows to be correct. In this sense, skepticism supports what the Lord has commanded us to do, which is to ask, seek, and knock (see D&C 88:63) or "to seek knowledge by study and also by faith" (D&C 88:118). In short, skepticism helps us fulfill the counsel of John, where we "believe not every spirit, but try the spirits whether they are of God: because many false prophets are gone out into the world" (1 John 4:1).

The weakness of skepticism is that if it becomes an identity unto itself, it can lead a person to reject everything that doesn't have sufficient evidence. This can produce two extremes: 1) you get someone who won't believe anything until he or she is made to personally witness it; or 2) you get a conspiracy theorist who skeptically rejects recognized authorities in lieu of special actors who alone possess the relevant facts. This particular tool has a way of promoting priestcraft at both ends of the continuum. What is common is that smart and diligent students of facts and information—in science and in history—find power and influence in knowing more about something than the layman and then use that information as a hammer against other people's beliefs. In both cases, the skeptic becomes a cynic and rejects what is right for what is preferred by his or her particular tribe.

Skeptics can also wield damage to members of the Church who are not settled in what they know and believe and who do not have reliable methods for accessing and verifying information. Many anti-Christs in the Book of Mormon (Nehor, Korihor, and Zeezrom) argued along skeptical lines of thought. The arguments were powerful and were only thwarted by individuals who knew how to defend against such attacks because of their identity as children of God.

Alma the Younger was someone who once went "about seeking to destroy the church of God" (Mosiah 27:10) employing skepticism to do so. The record tells us that he "was numbered among the unbelievers," "was a man of many words," and "led many of the people to do after the manner of his iniquities . . . stealing away the hearts of the people" (Mosiah 27:8–9). Skepticism appears to be one of Alma's primary tools to lead away the people. I suspect this on account of what the angel said who came to stop Alma and his brethren from destroying the church of God: "I have come to convince thee of the power and authority of God. . . . Now Behold, can ye dispute the power of God? For behold, doth not my voice shake the earth? And can ye not also behold me before you? And I am sent from God."

The angel's reference to the reality of his person and the effects of his power upon Alma and his brethren seem to be addressing a skeptical argument Alma had deployed to the people of the church—an argument that assailed the lack of evidence for 1) God's power manifest in the historical record; and 2) the reality of angels in the historical record. Alma apparently was skeptical of such things.

Figure 11: Summary of Skepticism

Skepticism	Strengths/Weaknesses	Examples
Rejection of all ideas and assertions for which there is contrary or insufficient warrant, support, or evidence.	**Strengths** Allows one to avoid being fooled. It is a tool for comparing new information with beliefs. **Weaknesses** Overt skepticism can encourage rejection of what is right in exchange for what is popular.	Resistance of new government programs that promise to ameliorate complex society ills. Tendency to support conspiracy theories in lieu of official accounts, such as John F. Kennedy, landing on the moon, rigged elections, and medication safety. Atheists who proselytize, such as the late Christopher Hitchens.

As it turns out, our Heavenly Father has endowed each of His children who are of normal mental capacity with a way of knowing, independent of any other source; including people. It is the seventh tool called conscience. Conscience is the ability to determine whether something is right and good, and therefore true, from something that is wrong and not true. The Lord revealed to Joseph Smith, "And the Spirit giveth light to every man that cometh into the world" (D&C 84:46), and "I [Lord] am the true light that lighteth every man that cometh into the world" (D&C 93:2). The light of conscience allows all men to know something is right and true without needing to have the knowledge confirmed by another person. It is a way of initially knowing the fundamentals about what is right and what is wrong, though this light can be dimmed by the corroding effects of one's upbringing or moral environment. An example of this occurs with King Lamoni in the Book of Mormon. Recall that it was "the tradition of Lamoni, which he had received from his father, that there was a Great Spirit. Notwithstanding they believed in a Great Spirit, they supposed that whatsoever they did was right; nevertheless, Lamoni began to fear exceedingly, with fear lest he had done wrong in slaying his servants" (Alma 18:5). Lamoni knew that murder was not right despite the accepted tradition that "whatsoever they did was right." For each of us, regardless of when and where we were born, it is conscience that supplies this knowledge to each of us.

When conscience is honored, men and women can exercise their agency to make choices that align with its demands. Because no person makes their decisions with the same set of information, it is conscience that enables the Lord to provide customized paths of mortality for each of His children. Conscience ensures that we can be judged based on our circumstances and provides accommodations to ensure that the Lord's judgment is just upon us—which in reality, we will all acknowledge before the judgment bar of God (see Alma 12:14–15).

If not for the plan of redemption, conscience would possess a downside: once men and women come to acknowledge and honor their conscience, they will simultaneously conclude that not all of their desires or actions have been good. They see that they have acted contrary to the light that was in them and that they have no way, of themselves, to make restitution. No person can change his or her own nature, which is fallen, without the help of God. A way has to be provided for men and women to be brought into alignment with conscience and, in time, change their natures to one that they prefer over all other influences. And, as mentioned, our Heavenly Father's plan of redemption—Jesus Christ—provides a way to reconcile ourselves to Him, who is the light within each of us:

> And the light which shineth, which giveth you light, is through him who enlighteneth your eyes, which is the same light that quickeneth your understandings; which light proceeedeth forth from the presence of God to fill the immensity of space—the light which is in all things, which giveth life to all things, which is the law by which all things are goverened, even the power of God who sitteth upon his throne, who is the bosom of eternity, who is in the midst of all things. (D&C 88:11–13)

Figure 12: Summary of Conscience

Conscience	Strengths/Weaknesses	Examples
The ability to distinguish good thoughts and actions that are true from acts and thoughts that are unrighteous and false.	**Strengths** 1) It ensures that all men of normal functioning mind can determine and decide what they believe and know among the choices of good and evil. 2) Allows for diversity of belief because each individual decides with different sets of information. 3) It reveals desires by their choices, or their character. This forced choice is called the agency of man. **Weaknesses** Once men realize that their desires are not all good, there is nothing they can do in and of themselves to change their heart.	Enos Alma Sr. Alma the Younger Sons of Mosiah King Lamoni Sr King Lamoni Jr. Zeezrom Corianton

Whereas conscience is hard-wired into each of us upon arrival into mortality, and all other tools can be accessed through the use of our minds and senses, the eighth tool is accessed through faith in God and righteousness and is called personal revelation.

God can and does communicate to all of His children according to His own will and pleasure. But to gain constant guidance to personal revelation, one must submit to the terms of redemption, including faith in Christ, repentance for sins committed against conscience, baptism by immersion for the remission of sins, and receiving the gift of the Holy Ghost through the laying on of hands of a legal administrator.

In the Doctrine and Covenants we learn, "And the Spirit giveth light to every man that cometh into the world [conscience]; and the Spirit enlighteneth every man through the world, that hearkeneth to the voice of the Spirit. And every one that hearkeneth to the voice of the Spirit (conscience) cometh unto God even the Father (via Jesus

Christ and his gospel 'I am the way, the truth, and the light, no man cometh unto Father but by me' (John 10:14)). And the Father teacheth him of the covenant which he has renewed and confirmed upon you, which is confirmed upon you for your sakes, and not for your sakes only, but for the sake of the whole world" (D&C 84:46–48).

Personal revelation is the most comprehensive way of knowing—in its immediacy, clarity, and convincing power. Unlike other tools of knowing, personal revelation requires no other witness, evidence, or testimony to know. Put simply, you feel that it is right as the mind and heart are filled with light and truth.

Personal revelation demands the most of us because revelations come subtly and so frequently that we may either ignore or miss them entirely. We ignore them when we feel inspired to act in a particular way—however small or inconvenient—and then fail to respond. We miss them or dismiss them when we rationalize impressions and feelings as our own making or from some other source. Despite our almost superstar ability to ignore and dismiss personal revelations, the Lord in His mercy and long-suffering continues patiently to "lead us along."

"And ye cannot bear all things now; nevertheless, be of good cheer, for I will lead you along. The kingdom is yours and the blessings thereof are yours, and the riches of eternity are yours." (D&C 78:18)

The Lord is not the only influence providing revelations to the minds and hearts of men and women on earth. The scriptures attest that the adversary of our souls—even Lucifer, Satan, the devil—can and does provide revelations to confuse, distract, and lead us away from the Lord. Satan's revelations do not carry with them the compelling and immediate influence of the Holy Ghost. His revelations are honed to flatter and enflame specific preferences of our thoughts and actions until we succumb to them. His approach is a sophisticated type of artificial intelligence borne from careful observation and successful entrapment. He plays upon facets of identity that we prefer above our child of God identity to enslave us to his will.

The scriptures speak of his revelations as "the power of the devil" (Jacob 7:4). The power of the devil entices us to prioritize our physical desires, passions, and appetites, inherent within the natural man above the commandments of God and conscience. The objective of Satan's revelations are that men and women "may get gain and praise of the world" (2 Nephi 26:29). Satan's revelations attack the way we think and attempt to influence what we spend our time thinking about. "And my vineyard," said the Lord to Joseph Smith, "has become corrupted every whit; and there is none which doeth good save it be a few; and they err in many instances because of priestcrafts, all having corrupt minds" (D&C 33:4).

The challenge of personal revelation is striving to receive revelations in righteousness, while also actively watching out for revelations from Satan to our mind and heart that attempt to lure us away from the covenant path. Satan lures us subtley—with a flaxen cord, so that if we are not on constant lookout we can be led astray "carefully down to hell" (2 Nephi 28:21–24).

Figure 13: Summary of Personal Revelation

Personal Revelation	Strengths/Weaknesses	Examples
Ideas, directives, and feelings that come from the unseen world.	**Strengths** Personal revelation is the most powerful way of knowing; encompassing and exceeding all the other ways of knowing. **Weaknesses** Difficult to always accept revelations of God and reject all revelations from Satan.	Many examples where extreme emphasis is placed upon principles that are true but are held as absolute to the point that they become disconnected from other gospel principles and doctrines.

The last tool of knowing is what we learn from our environment through the unspoken norms of doing and believing. Norms are usually recognized once they are violated. Those who witness the breach are shocked if not offended. These moments cause immediate backlash and are often cringeworthy. Norms can be a positive and negative force depending on what they sustain or hold in place. Societal norms from the 1950s governing sexually explicit behavior, the role of men in society, crude language, and attitudes toward the elderly are examples of positive norms that once regulated societal behavior. Over time, as these norms eroded, new norms emerged that normalized behavior and speech previously considered deviant. The new norms help ensure society does not revert back to its former patterns of decency and modesty.

The tool of social knowledge involves two primary methods of control, namely science and history. As with the other tools of knowledge, both science and history provide benefits and weaknesses when used to ascertain the truth. It is essential to understand the limitations of each in order to think clearly about our identities as children of God and to effectively quarantine the influence of competing facets of identity.

SCIENCE

Science describes our physical surroundings and the universe in rational terms. By rational, we mean that the explanation has to be internally consistent and agree with the specific requirements that govern scientific thought. The requirements governing scientific thought include certain facts, laws, theories, and postulates that sustain and reinforce one another.

Scientific facts are data that an observer identifies and shares with others based upon his beliefs, observations, and prolonged interactions with the subject. The observer theorizes about his or her observations and discoveries and applies a variety of methods to establish validity. Usually, the postulates of the observer will conform to his or her society. If the observer's facts are consistently and repeatedly discovered by others in separate observations, they are more likely to be accepted as true. Over time, "true" facts become laws. As scientific laws proliferate and interact with one another, observers use their minds to formulate theories to explain the regularities of nature. Thus, scientific theory invokes notions for which there is no direct observational acquaintance and are limited to the observations of humans to date. They are never complete because new observations are always underway. As theories gain popularity, they begin to harden into scientific postulates and even articles of faith[9]—postulates and articles that both guide and limit future theory construction in science.

---

9. C. Riddle, *Think Independently*, 56–57. "They are 'articles of faith' because they cannot be justified apart from the strength of the total scientific enterprise they enable. The most common are rationalism, least action, and naturalism."

HISTORY

History attempts to explain the past by creating a rational, verbal account of events. With that said, the primary purpose of history is to influence how we think and act now and in the future. In order for history to be considered valid and useful, the narrative must address certain fundamentals, namely continuants, which are the physical, observable artifacts from the past; and primary source documents, which are the main materials for reconstructing the past. Such documents may include eyewitness testimony (verbal or written) and secondary accounts. The best documents are those written at the time of the event, by people who witnessed or participated directly in the event and were without selfish motivations.[10] Secondary documents are useful but may have been written from memory at a later time or by people who heard the account from an eyewitness. The best sources are contemporary to the time an event occurred and are provided by a direct participant who was capable of understanding and accurately describing the event without bias or motivation to obscure details of the account. Generally speaking, there are far more secondary source documents that describe our history than primary source documentation.

Historians establish facts about the past based on their review of primary and secondary sources and historical continuants. Thus, historical facts are limited by one, the availability of historical sources and continuants; two, the ability of the historian to accurately interpret the information; and three, the limitations of the historian in envisioning a time and place in which he or she was not present. When trends or patterns are observed by many historians, scholars will eventually declare this or that conclusion to be a historical law. Like their scientific counterparts, historians use historical laws to invent theories to explain why things happen. Historical theories reflect consensus among historians, though they are subject to change as new information is discovered and integrated into the historical narrative.

---

10. "Decisions should be based upon qualified sources and free from selfish motivations" (D. Oaks, "Truth and the Plan," October 2018 general conference).

In order to challenge existing historical theory, every primary source must be accounted for. An additional postulate requires that any hypotheses about historical causes must be naturalistic. Finally, generally accepted history requires that no sources or continuants, primary or otherwise, be attributed to supernatural means.

Figure 14: Summary of Social Knowledge

Social Knowledge	Strengths/Weaknesses
Imposition of norms to control what is known and preferred within society: with science and history as the primary forms of control.	**Strengths** Ensures continuity of tacit and explicit knowledge over time with the possibility for expanding what is known. **Weaknesses** Postulates depend upon consensus of observations that almost always conform to societal norms.

REFLECTION

I invite you to consider the following questions about the tools of knowing and write down your reflections.

1. What is the relationship between the nine tools of knowing and our discussion on identity?
2. What tools do you find yourself using most frequently to know what you know?
3. Which tools, if any, would help you become more effective at knowing what is right and good instead of what is easy and available?
4. What is the relationship between the tools you use frequently and your primary identity?
5. Which tools do you rely upon to reinforce and safeguard your primary identity?
6. If your primary identity is not the child of God identity, are there tools that could help you change? Which ones? How would you begin to use them?

The nine tools of knowing help us recognize arguments that are true while reinforcing our efforts to discern truth from error and avoid deception. However, another challenge remains. If we are to be fully equipped, we must understand some of our limitations when it comes to thinking and perceiving data prior to its formation into an argument. To succeed, we must obtain proper perspective by getting above the argumentative fray. What we need is a ladder.

CHAPTER 3

Ladders, Ripples, and Rocks

As discussed previously, our identities—and their many facets—are consequences of how we choose to act, what we choose to believe, and the attachment we feel with others who have chosen similarly to us. Changing our identity requires that we make different choices—choices that prioritize different beliefs and actions and that result in a preferred attachment to alternative ways of viewing the world. In short, we choose identities, and we can change them. However, the path to changing our identities is compromised because our identity affects the data upon which we focus in our environment and the meaning we attribute to it. If we are to alter our identity, we must first come to see our surroundings differently. The problem is a cognitive problem. Fortunately, we have a tool to help us. It is called the Ladder of Inference.[1]

THE LADDER

The Ladder of Inference (See Figure 15) is a metaphor to help us compare our actions to the beliefs we profess to those we actually practice. Researchers have found that a person's behavior is best explained by the mental models they hold. Mental models are cognitive paradigms that guide how a person sees the world. For our purposes, mental models are equated to a person's primary identity. The ladder helps a person evaluate the steps we take from the time one first selects data from their environment all the way to acting upon their beliefs.

---

1. Argyris and Schon, *Organizational Learning II: Theory, Method, and Practice* (Reading, Massachusetts: Addison-Wesley, 1996).

Figure 15: Ladder of Inference

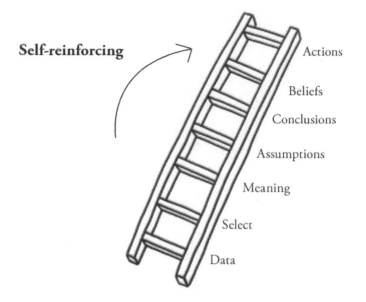

At the base of the ladder is a pool of data representing all of the available information of a person's environment. The ladder starts with the rung of selection, which the person ascends when he or she chooses to focus upon certain information and consider it valuable. Once information is selected, the person takes the next step up the ladder to the rung of meaning. Here, one attributes meaning to the selected data. The meaning assigned to the data is a reflection of the values that we hold, those most important to us. Our values lead us to the next step on the ladder, the step of assumption. Our values carry certain assumptions about what is right and what is wrong, what provides benefit and what is a detriment. Our assumptions likewise lead us to certain conclusions about the data we have focused on. Conclusions are the forerunner to our decisions about how the world works and the way things are and should be. In short, our conclusions form the basis for our beliefs. And our beliefs lead us to action. They are the fuel to our behavior.

It is important to note that the ladder leads us to climb toward the values and beliefs of our primary identities, *not the identities we espouse.* So, another clue to discovering your primary identity is to consider *how you actually behave, not what you believe.* It is not always easy to see the disparity between what we espouse and what we do, but we can—sometimes with others help—increase our capacity to assess the gap accurately. Every time we encounter a new situation we have never responded to, we take a few steps down the ladder to make fresh assumptions. We then re-ascend, based on those assumptions. That sounds good until we realize that our choices are continually limited because we never get past our primary identity-driven assumptions!

Life on the ladder is dynamic, but the challenge is how to climb down far enough to see information with a perspective that allows us to attribute different meaning than that required by our primary identity. If we wish to choose a new identity, we must learn to come all the way down the ladder. Only by descending to the bottom can we select different data and attribute new meaning to it. This can be very difficult because our primary identities do not surrender their ground easily. Still, we have been told that we have the power to invite such transformations into our lives: "For verily I say, men should be anxiously engaged in a good cause, and do many things of their own free will, and bring to pass much righteousness; *for the power is in them, wherein they are agents unto themselves.* And inasmuch as men do good they shall in nowise lose their reward" (D&C 58:27–28; emphasis added).

To help illustrate how the ladder works, let us use an example from an individual in the scriptures referenced earlier: Peter, son of Jonas and Apostle of Jesus. Use your own answers to the questions concerning Peter (at the end of chapter 1) as a starting point. There are no right or wrong answers here because only God and Peter can tell us what Peter considered as his primary identity at the time these events occurred.

Based on the information in the scriptures, it appears that Peter's primary identity was still that of a fisherman, no doubt a consequence of his professional, cultural, and familial heritage. I say that because of his statement, when confronted with uncertainty and stress resulting from Jesus's death, "to go a fishing" (see John 21:3–7, 9, 15–17). Peter was still in the process of anchoring his primary identity as a child of God, and the pull as a fisherman, or more specifically as the son of a fisherman, challenged him. On the water, casting out and drawing in nets, was where Peter felt most comfortable. Preaching and teaching were out of his comfort zone. In spite of what Peter believed and felt prior to this moment—the powerful witness of Jesus that he shared on multiple occasions, for instance—he was still a son of Jonas first and a child of God second, which is why I think the Savior continually addressed him this way when questioning him. To be a son of Jonas was to embrace the beliefs, attitudes, assumptions, and behaviors learned from his father. It was to see the world through a lens where laboring for your daily meat was the most important activity of the day, and the size of the haul was the ultimate sign of success.[2]

Jesus's questioning of Peter invited him to come down the ladder and reconsider some of his actions and the beliefs that drove them. To Peter, Jesus asked, "Simon, son of Jonas, lovest thou me *more than these*?" (John 21:15; emphasis added). Jesus is probing into Peter's espoused beliefs and inviting him to reprioritize his identity. When Peter responds, "Yea, Lord, thou knowest that I love thee," Jesus draws attention to Peter's behavioral gap—between his "espoused belief" and his "belief in action"—by saying, "Feed my lambs." Lambs are baby sheep. Caring for lambs, namely believers who are young in their knowledge of the gospel and in need of nourishment, requires Peter to be engaged early and often. Otherwise, those lambs will starve. In order for Peter to truly love Jesus first, he needs to consider how his actions are not always aligned with the "early/often" requirement of taking care of lambs. Peter steps back down the ladder to the rung of belief.

To revisit his beliefs, Peter needs to consider the conclusions he has drawn about the necessity to fish. He has judged fishing activities to be of highest value, to be attended to fully, or else, how will one survive? Perhaps reading Peter's mind, Jesus asks him again, "Simon, son of Jonas"—again, using the Apostle's birth name and identity, as opposed to his new name of Peter—"lovest thou me?" Peter responds, "Yea, Lord; thou knowest that I love thee. [Jesus] saith unto him, Feed my sheep" (John 21:16). Sheep are fully grown, but they, too, need to be fed. They, too, are in need of constant nourishment. And it is again Peter's job to feed them. Lest he conclude that maybe, after he has fed the lambs, there will be time to fish—an assumption that fishing is

---

2. Jeffrey R. Holland, "The First Great Commandment," *Ensign*, November 2012. The pile of fish was 153, a stunning haul that would have really challenged Peter's long held assumptions about successful fishing.

always an important task—Jesus reiterates that fishing is not part of the program. Peter steps down to the rung of meaning. He must now ask himself a series of questions:

> What meaning did I attribute to fishing that led to my conclusions and judgments of how the world worked? In the grand scheme of things, did I make fishing out to be of higher value than it is? It was my father's profession, I fed my family and others, and earned a living doing so. I have become expert at it; I have taught my own children how to do it, and do it well. And I really am good at it and enjoy it. But then again, perhaps I have made it too important, and placed it ahead of weightier things. After all, it led me here, and one thing is clear, the Lord is not pleased that I am back here.

According to Jeffrey R. Holland, the Lord's response to Peter might have sounded something like this:

> Peter, why are you here? Why are we back on this same shore, by these same nets, having this same conversation? Wasn't it obvious then and isn't it obvious now that if I want fish, I can get fish? What I need, Peter, are disciples—and I need them forever. I need someone to feed my sheep and save my lambs. I need someone to preach my gospel and defend my faith. I need someone who loves me, truly, truly loves me, and loves what our Father in Heaven has commissioned me to do. Ours is not a feeble message. It is not a fleeting task. It is not hapless; it is not hopeless; it is not to be consigned to the ash heap of history. It is the work of Almighty God, and it is to change the world. So, Peter, for the second and presumably the last time, I am asking you to leave all this and to go teach and testify, labor and serve loyally until the day in which they will do to you exactly what they did to me.[3]

Now that Peter has come down the ladder and reassessed the meaning he chose—yes, it was a cultural and familial inheritance, but

---

3. Ibid., 84.

chosen it was nonetheless—he is empowered to see the world around him with new eyes, through a different filter, even the child of God filter. This filter changes everything, of course, "shaping the history of the world in which we now live."[4]

RIPPLES

The ladder helps us reconsider the influences of our facets of identity and enables us to ensure that the child of God identity is at the primary position. As was the case with Peter, we may assume we already have made the child of God identity primary. But as was the case with him, we undoubtedly have a lot of work to do. Like the ladder, another tool is available to help us see the world more clearly before we attribute meaning to our area of focus. The tool is familiar to all of us: ripples.

As indicated earlier, the Ladder of Influence sits in a pool of data, at least metaphorically (Figure 16).

Figure 16. The Ladder in a Pool of Data with Ripples

Available Data Pool

Any pool, when disturbed by an object or by wind, leaves ripples. In our model, ripples are evidence or trace of activity within the data. Sometimes, we cause the ripples ourselves by interacting with the

---

4. Ibid.

data, and so we know what caused them. But other times we don't see what caused the ripples. We just know by their presence that something disturbed the surface.

One of our tendencies as humans is to ascend the ladder quickly, based on an initial and minor scan of the data pool. We do so because it helps us make rapid decisions for the thousands of daily decisions that govern our lives. But such rapid decision-making also means that many of our decisions become automatic and habitual, occurring for the most part in the background of our minds. This results in patterns of action that are not only less scrutinized but may be wrong or incongruent with the values we espouse. Over time, this tendency can lead us to come to know much information that is simply not correct or true. Paying attention to the ripples—even their very presence—in our data pool helps us scrutinize our selection processes before we ascend the ladder and give the data we observe meaning. Ripples are, therefore, signals to become better selectors of information.

Ripples are also evidence of something that occurred in the environment but was never observed. Within the framework of knowing via science and history, postulates, theories, and facts are established based on evidence and continuants that can be observed, measured, and analyzed directly. Neither science nor history naturally accommodate for evidence that cannot be observed directly. This means that their methods do not naturally try to explain and account for ripples. In this situation, we need tools for knowing such as rationalism or revelation are needed to fill in the gaps. If a person's identity leads them to focus on only a selection of tools of knowing, or even rejects the validity of certain tools from the outset, it will be impossible to gather and evaluate enough information to avoid a condition of rebellion or unbelief.

Consider an example. Plural marriage was revealed to Joseph Smith as early as 1832, but beginning in 1841, it was practiced in earnest by relatively few individuals.[5] Joseph Smith left no account of his motivation

---

5. See Gospel Topics Essays: "Plural Marriage in The Church of Jesus Christ of Latter-day Saints," https://www.churchofjesuschrist.org/study/manual/gospel -topics-essays/plural-marriage-in-the-church-of-jesus-christ-of-latter-day -saints?lang=eng.

for instituting the practice, no reason the Lord commanded it,[6] and no statement on his experience obeying the practice. These facts are an example of an object entering into the data pool and creating ripples. Historians are dependent upon the ripples to theorize about Joseph's motives, intentions, and rationale for practicing plural marriage as they apply their methods to create a narrative that adequately takes into account primary and secondary sources from those closest to Joseph.

Based on what is known today, it would appear that historians have accounted for every primary testimony and second hand sources from individuals who practiced plural marriage during Joseph Smith's lifetime. Depending on the identity of the historian, however, many different theories have been proposed about Joseph's motivations behind the teaching. Why isn't there consensus? I believe it is because certain historians fail to account for ripples that do not conform to their primary identities and their ascension up the ladder. Some see the volume of wives as evidence of an untamed sexual drive. Others see the ages of wives as evidence of tyrannical, sinister oppression. Still others see the marital status of women at the time he proposed as evidence of his deviancy and untruthfulness.

Each of these concerns is unwarranted, in my view, if a person comes back down the ladder, reflects upon his or her primary identity that attaches certain meaning to the data they have observed, and widens his or her aperture to consider all of the ripples left by Joseph. What ripples exist that explain more of Joseph Smith's sexual motivations? What are the testimonies of those who knew him? What have they said about his virtue, honor, and uprightness? These testimonies constitute ripples in the water that when rightly considered do much to provide a fuller picture of Joseph's motivations and character.

Ripples are a tool to help us as we climb our Ladders of Inference and strive to more fully acquire the child of God identity. Ripples invite us to pause, come back down the ladder, and gather more evidence before we assign meaning. Additionally, ripples give us space to deal with facts that are unknown, widening our view to consider even more facts,

---

6. D&C 132 provides some implication for the rationale but as a revelation, given in prophetic voice, it is not the same as Joseph explaining it directly.

some that may not have been considered within a scientific or historical frame of knowing. In short, ripples help us live with patience and faith.

There are times, however, when not even ripples are enough to answer certain questions definitively. In such cases, a rock is helpful.

ROCK

In the scriptures, rocks are symbols of wisdom, which means correctly applying truth in one's life. In His Sermon on the Mount, Jesus taught the multitude that it was upon a rock that they were to build their spiritual homes so that "when the rains descended, and the floods came, and the winds blew, and beat upon that house; and it fell not for it was found upon a rock" (Matthew 7:25). Luke records the teaching slightly differently, emphasizing both the depth a person must dig to build a house upon a rock foundation and the benefit such a foundation would provide towards not being shaken: "He is like a man which built an house, and digged deep, and laid the foundation on a rock; and when the flood arose, the stream beat vehemently upon that house, and could not shake it: for it was founded upon a rock" (Luke 6:48).

The Book of Mormon explains more completely the importance of rocks in keeping our spiritual homes protected, while identifying the reason why this is so. Nephi, son of Helaman, testified to his sons on this very point:

> And now, my sons, remember, remember that it is upon the rock of our Redeemer, who is Christ, the Son of God, that ye must build your foundation; that when the devil shall send forth his mighty winds, yea, his shafts in the whirlwind, yea, when all his hail and his mighty storm shall beat upon you, it shall have no power over you to drag you down to the gulf of misery and endless wo, *because of the rock upon which ye are built,* which is a sure foundation, a foundation whereon if men build they cannot fall.[7] (Helaman 5:12; emphasis added)

---

7. The Savior also explained that His gospel is His rock and to accept it into your life is the equivalent in building upon Him directly (see 3 Nephi 11:39, 18:12–13; D&C 11:16; 33:13).

Rocks matter because the rock is Jesus Christ and His gospel, which helps us live with patience and faith while knowing what is right and true.

Building our foundation upon the rock of Jesus's gospel implies that we use this rock to compare both what we know and what we don't know. Recall in chapter 3 (see Figure 4) that when it comes to the gospel, we believe much more than what has actually been revealed; and what we believe consists of things that are true and things that are false—with some portion of what we believe and have come to know that is true, and some that is false. As we scan the data pool of information, we must always be asking ourselves, a few key questions:

- Is this information consistent with what the Lord has revealed?
- Can I find examples in the scriptures or the teachings of prophets to support what I see, hear, or feel?
- Does my interpretation of this data or information align with the collective statements of the First Presidency and Quorum of the Twelve Apostles?

Building on the Rock requires each of us to answer these questions in the affirmative and behave accordingly.

Several years ago, a Church employee shared (in truth, it was leaked) a slide that summarized the primary reasons members of the Church build their spiritual residence somewhere other than on the rock of the gospel. The slide looked something like this:

Figure 17. Issues Leading People to Build on Sandy Foundations

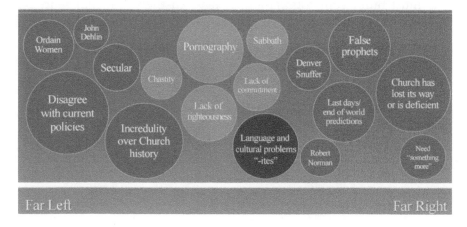

The issues mentioned in the slide are situated along a liberal/conservative continuum, with those issues considered to be preferred by members with more liberal beliefs on the left, and issues more appealing to members with conservative beliefs on the right. The size of the circles represents the relative appeal of the issue to members who leave the Church. Some issues are matters of policy, some are preference for specific behavior, and others are preference for the teachings and influence of select individuals.

When considering these issues separately, which, if any, do you think completely align with what is contained in the scriptures or the consensus teachings of Church leaders? By my estimation, the answer is none; all of them fail to meet this requirement. The rock is helpful, therefore, in helping us sift away personality, thoughts, and influence that are often mingled together with gospel truths. In each case, if a person were to apply information coming from one or more of these sources to what is taught in the scriptures and living prophets collectively, they would know that such teachings are not true and are not to be believed or accepted. The rock is a sure defense in keeping our houses unshaken, just as the Savior promised it would.

Jacob, the brother of Nephi, built his house upon the rock. In Jacob 7, he recounts an experience he had with Sherem, an anti-Christ, who came among the people of Nephi:

> [Sherem] came among the people . . . and began to preach . . . and declare that there should be no Christ. And he preached many things which were flattering unto the people . . . and he labored diligently that he might lead away the hearts of the people, insomuch that he did lead away many hearts . . . and he was learned, that he had a perfect knowledge of the language of the people; wherefore, he could use much flattery, and much power of speech, according to the power of the devil. And he had hope to shake me from the faith. (Jacob 7:1–6)

What tools of knowing does Sherem emphasize to gain credibility with the people of Nephi? What can we imagine Sherem's identity to be given his apparent reliance on such tools? If you were to meet

Sherem and he looked for an opportunity to seek you out and challenge you, what tools of knowing would you rely on? Here is what Jacob did: "He had hope to shake me from the faith notwithstanding the revelations and the many things which I had seen concerning these things; for I truly had seen angels, and they had ministered unto me. And also I had heard the voice of the Lord speaking unto me in very word, from time to time; wherefore, I could not be shaken" (Jacob 7:5).

What tools of knowing did Jacob rely on? How did such tools inform his identity? What identity do you suppose Jacob to hold? How did his preferred tools of knowing help him build his foundation on the rock of Jesus Christ? How might they help you?

CHAPTER 4

Learning by Revelation

D&C 8:2–3

As mentioned in chapter 2, revelation from God to each of us is the best way to know whether an idea is correct and good and, therefore, worthy of acceptance. Revelations from God are presented to us through two primary channels: through living prophets (what has been described as the priesthood channel) and to our minds and hearts from the Holy Ghost (what has been described as the personal channel).[1]

PERSONAL AND PRIESTHOOD CHANNELS OF REVELATION

The two channels differ from one another in a few fundamental ways. First, the personal channel is the channel we use to know what is right.[2] Both channels present us with information for consideration, but only the personal channel can provide us with knowledge. Understanding this is essential to fully accepting the child of God identity. Second, continual guidance (not episodic manifestations) via the personal channel is inseparably linked with righteousness.

---

1. Dallin H. Oaks, "Two Lines of Communication," *Ensign*, October 2010.
2. "This personal line of communication with our Heavenly Father through His Holy Spirit is the source of our testimony of truth, of our knowledge, and of our personal guidance from a loving Heavenly Father. It is an essential feature of His marvelous gospel plan, which allows each one of His children to receive a personal witness of its truth" (Ibid., 83).

By righteousness, I mean behavior that is aligned with revealed truth from God. Our Heavenly Father can and does provide personal guidance in times of need to His sons and daughters, but only to individuals who are continually striving to keep God's commandments and renewing their desire to "always have his spirit to be with them" (D&C 20:77, 79) does He provide constant, reliable direction. Members can compare the inspiration they are receiving through their personal channel with the commandments of God and know to what extent that their inspiration is from Him and to what extent it is coming from some other source. Regarding this principle, Elder Oaks has taught: "Unfortunately, it is common for persons who are violating God's commandments or disobedient to the counsel of their priesthood leaders to declare that God has revealed to them that they are excused from obeying some commandment or from following some counsel. Such persons may be receiving revelation or inspiration, but it is not from the source they suppose."[3]

A third way that the personal revelatory channel differs from the priesthood channel is that the priesthood channel introduces information to us through intermediaries, the Savior being our primary intermediary, and from Him to the prophets. This has implications for each of us because information presented through the priesthood channel requires us to process it the same as we would all other data. However, depending on our identity profile, we may be at risk of processing priesthood channel information in ways that are inconsistent with the child of God identity. We will say more about this later on.

Finally, it is only through the priesthood channel that we access information essential for exaltation.[4] The priesthood channel is an essential channel of drawing closer to Jesus Christ precisely because it is

---

3. Ibid., 84.
4. Ibid. "The priesthood line is the channel by which God has spoken to His children through the scriptures in times past. And it is this line through which He currently speaks through the teachings and counsel of living prophets and apostles and other inspired leaders. This is the way we receive the required ordinances. This is the way we receive calls to service in His Church. His Church is the way and His priesthood is the power through which we are privileged to participate in those cooperative activities that are essential to accomplishing the Lord's work. These include preaching the gospel, building temples and chapels, and helping the poor."

only through this channel that He introduces us to His gospel, ordinances, and church. From a nine tool of knowing perspective, it is an authoritarian channel that provides each of us opportunities to learn through pragmatic, empirical, rationalistic, and revelatory means.

Both channels (personal and priesthood) mutually reinforce one another, and we are reliant upon the Holy Ghost to know the truth of things presented to us via the priesthood channel.[5] Additionally, we are expected to use the nine tools of knowing to evaluate information from the priesthood channel and to exercise our moral agency in discerning between things that are right and true on the one hand and those that are beneficial but not essential to our individual exaltation on the other.

INCORRECT ASSUMPTIONS OF PERSONAL AND PRIESTHOOD REVELATORY CHANNELS

Depending upon one's identity makeup, it is possible—even common—to make incorrect assumptions about information flowing from both the personal and priesthood channel. For instance, some members mistakenly assume that personal sentiment and spiritual sensationalism come from the Holy Ghost (feelings/emotionalism). If we are not careful, such an assumption can lead us away from the covenant path.[6] Making such a conclusion assumes that unusual feelings are always a product of the Holy Ghost telling us something and that such feelings—no matter how or when they are received—must come from God. In order to know whether physical sensations are from God or not, we must come back down the ladder and evaluate the meaning we apply to them.

What we feel through our senses is a form of data at the base of our ladder. As with all data, we choose which feelings we will focus upon, or select, and then make another choice by giving it meaning. Correctly interpreting our feelings, whether they are from God or

---

5. Ibid., 85.

6. Joseph Smith taught, "Nothing is a greater injury to the children of men than to be under the influence of a false spirit, when they think they have the Spirit of God" (*Times and Seasons*, April 1, 1842, 744).

not, can be rationally and empirically tested by applying a companion test of evaluating the impact upon our mind (see D&C 8:2–3). Elder David A. Bednar taught that understanding—as used in the scriptures—is a revealed conclusion by the Holy Ghost.[7] Recall that our conclusions about what is right and true flow from our assumptions about the meaning we select and apply to them (see Figure 15 in chapter 3). The blessing of the Holy Ghost confirming something to our mind and our heart means that what we have assumed is, in fact, correct[8] and can be believed to be true and acted upon with confidence. However, if we move to belief and action based on this feeling alone, without the confirming and companion attestation from the Holy Ghost, we may be acting on feelings that are not right and good. We are then vulnerable to being led astray.

Consider this observation from Elder Bednar about acting upon information based on its logic or feeling alone:

> People may experience the patterns of coming to understand in their minds and hearts in different sequences. Sometimes the mind takes the lead, and the heart follows; sometimes the heart takes the lead, and the head follows. And sometimes mind and heart interact in distinctive and iterative ways. Ultimately, however, a person can end up at a desired spiritual destination—and mind and heart are aligned. The safeguard that helps prevent deception and misinterpretation is that true understanding requires both.[9]

---

7. "The scriptures tell us, "Apply thine heart to understanding" (Proverbs 2:2). This verse is interesting because typically we think of understanding things cognitively and rationally with our minds. But, as what we know in our mind is confirmed as true in our heart by the witness of the Holy Ghost, then we are blessed with understanding. Thus, understanding is a revealed conclusion and a spiritual gift" (D. Bednar, *The Spirit of Revelation* [Salt Lake City: Deseret Book, 2021], 4).

8. Sometimes the Holy Ghost reveals a conclusion to us that is contrary to assumptions we hold about the world or things around us. Provided such revelations align to the scriptures and general revelations from living prophets, such occurrences can be trusted as valid and are one of the best ways to identify facets of our identity that need to be evaluated.

9. Ibid., 5.

Understanding from the Holy Ghost that reaches both the mind and heart is the primary way to know whether our feelings alone are right and good and revealed from God.

Another incorrect assumption about the personal and priesthood channel occurs when a person assumes that information through the priesthood channel is equivalent to a requirement to believe in some "thing." On its face, this assumption may seem absolute—which it is in many cases but not in all cases. For instance, consider all of the information that comes from the Lord to His prophets. In today's day and age, the information to which they provide their stamp of approval varies widely. They teach us the doctrines of the gospel; issue policies to administer the Church; approve adult, youth, and children programs; oversee publications and media campaigns; contribute to legislation; and a host of other endeavors. How should we view such information? Should we make distinctions between information that is for our benefit from information that should command our allegiance? If so, what can we use to guide us?

The task is made easier if we acknowledge that there is much information currently given to us through the priesthood channel that we are not required to accept as true, however beneficial and well intended it might be. By "true," I mean information that commands not only our support but also our belief and obedience. A few examples will help explain what I mean.

Brigham Young University–Provo and BYU–Idaho are both Church-owned schools with the same board of trustees, namely the First Presidency and Quorum of the Twelve Apostles. And yet, these schools have differing dress codes. At BYU–Idaho, a female cannot where capri pants, while at BYU–Provo, a student can wear capris, even shorts. The dress code at both campuses is aligned with principles of modesty and consistent with the university honor codes, but neither code constitutes a "true" way to dress for all members of the Church.

Another example is found in the Church social media campaign "I'm a Mormon," which was utilized worldwide after the turn of the century. Many of us participated in the campaign to build greater community awareness of Church members' lives and beliefs. The campaign went on for a few years before ending. A few years later,

President Nelson announced renewed focus and emphasis on using the full name of the Lord's Church in all publications and communications.[10] The "I'm a Mormon" campaign did not constitute a "true" campaign, even though it was approved, endorsed, and directed by the Lord's prophets. It, like so many other directives, was subject to change and adaptation as circumstances required. It is my belief that it was the will of the Lord at the time. But what the Lord wills in one circumstance might be completely different from what He requires in another. Therefore, I can acknowledge the campaign as the Lord's will but not feel compelled to believe that what I am supporting constitutes truth in and of itself. I can maintain my own beliefs on how best to manage a campaign and whether to and to what degree I will participate, while still supporting the effort completely.

A final example is seen in the recent updates to the Church's official handbook, which describes official policies and required actions to guide the Lord's Church. The handbook is not "true" because future updates will most certainly occur, as has been the case since the Church was restored. The policies contained in the handbook are certainly the Lord's will for members to whom they apply (there are geographic differences in many policies), but it is precisely because they will change and because they don't universally apply to all that we recognize them for what they are: policies adapted to the time, geography, and circumstance of the Church's members. Therefore, we climb down our ladders and attribute different meaning to such things than we do to other types of information that flows through the priesthood channel. We recognize that such information is not binding upon us and does not affect our eternal exaltation, even though we actively sustain it as the will of the Lord. The child of God identity is what allows us to make such distinctions in the information. Meanwhile, other competing identities—such as "member of the Lord's Church," do not.[11]

---

10. See Russell M. Nelson, "The Correct Name of the Church," *Ensign*, October, 2018.

11. It is important to acknowledge that the child of God identity is not an amorphous, catch-all term, to anything related to the gospel of Jesus Christ. There are, in my opinion, many identities closely related to the child of God identity

DOCTRINE VERSUS OTHER
FORMS OF INFORMATION

How do the constructs covered in this book relate to one's thinking about Church doctrines versus other forms of information, such as Church policy? Is there a difference? As previously noted, policies are adapted to circumstances of members and change frequently, meaning their rate of change is more aligned with societal change. In addition, policies are not found within the scriptures, though the principles upon which policies are based most certainly are. This can make them more difficult to distinguish from doctrines that require our allegiance and to which we should strive for individual knowledge from the Holy Ghost.[12]

For many of us, our stances on social issues are strongly influenced by the political identity we embrace. Like all competing identities, our political identities require us to think and act in certain ways, even if such thinking is contrary to information from the priesthood channel. Some examples of the kinds of policies that can distinguish political identities include caring for the poor, elderly, and displaced; providing welfare support for the unemployed, underemployed, or disadvantaged; views toward gender dysphoria, abortion, and taxation. For

---

but have requirements of thought and action which are not consistent with the Lord's revelations to the prophets. It is impossible to name or label all such identities, but someone who places their membership (as referenced here) in the organization of the Church ahead of the child of God identity is someone who might struggle with commandments of God which require inclusion and compassion ahead of membership norms, for example.

12. D. Oaks, "Divine Love in the Father's Plan," *Ensign*, April, 2022. Elder Oaks uses "The Family: A Proclamation to the World" as an example of the difference between policies which can be changed and doctrines which cannot: "A uniquely valuable teaching to help us prepare for eternal life, 'the greatest of all the gifts of God,' is the 1995 proclamation on the family. Its declarations are, of course, different from some current laws, practices, and advocacy, such as cohabitation and same-sex marriage. Those who do not fully understand the Father's loving plan for His children may consider this family proclamation no more than a changeable statement of policy. In contrast, we affirm that the family proclamation, founded on irrevocable doctrine, defines the kind of family relationships where the most important part of our eternal development can occur."

many, what is assumed to be "right" and "true" for all Church members politically is a reflection of their own political identity. However, national and political party issues—just like Church policy—can and does differ for many political issues across countries, so we must use caution not to use Church policies (authoritarian argument) as justification for our political beliefs—beliefs that are often based on faulty assumptions of what is "right" or "the Lord's will." We should remember the recent caution from President Oaks, who said:

> There are many political issues, and no party, platform, or individual candidate can satisfy all personal preferences. Each citizen must therefore decide which issues are most important to him or her at any particular time. Then members should seek inspiration on how to exercise their influence according to their individual priorities. This process will not be easy. It may require changing party support or candidate choices, even from election to election. Such independent actions will sometimes require voters to support candidates or political parties or platforms whose other positions they cannot approve. That is one reason we encourage our members to refrain from judging one another in political matters. We should never assert that a faithful Latter-day Saint cannot belong to a particular party or vote for a particular candidate. We teach correct principles and leave our members to choose how to prioritize and apply those principles on the issues presented from time to time.[13]

When priesthood channels deliver information that isn't doctrinally based, we are expected to use the nine tools to determine which issues are "right" and "good," and then avoid grasping any information too tightly that could easily change in the future or that isn't currently required of all members everywhere. The child of God identity provides the greatest latitude to believe all that has been revealed without fear of being condemned by the Lord.

---

13. Dallin H. Oaks, "Defending Our Divinely Inspired Constitution," *Ensign*, April, 2021.

RECOGNIZING INFORMATION THAT REQUIRES OUR ALLEGIANCE

Some information through priesthood channels is vital and requires our belief and sustaining behavior, as mental ascent for such doctrines is not enough. We are not required to know all of these things yet, only to believe them and strive to know them until the Lord sees fit to reveal their truth to us personally.

Information that requires our allegiance can be thought of as general revelations, meaning they require the same actions from all people everywhere. There are no country-to-country adaptations for these revelations, and no one is exempt. In addition, general revelations are not difficult to recognize. This is because prophets will announce them as such and teach them collectively and repeatedly. Unlike policies and other forms of information adapted to time, geography, and circumstance, general revelations do not change unless the Lord no longer requires them, in which case He would reveal discontinuance of them directly. Their constancy and clarity, therefore, can be relied upon by all members everywhere.

General revelations from the Lord are received through priesthood channels only, beginning with the First Presidency and Quorum of the Twelve Apostles. The revelations they receive are aligned with their apostolic stewardship, which in turn applies to every man and woman upon on the earth. In addition, general revelations are governed by priesthood keys and reside in formal offices of the Church[14] in a similar manner as one receives personal revelations—meaning through the feelings, thoughts, and impressions confirmed to the mind and heart via the Holy Ghost. And because revelations for the entire Church are received by fifteen men collectively, there is great safety for members of the Church.

One reason this is so is contained in the Lord's requirement for each Apostle to receive the same answer before action is taken. Unanimity in decision-making is the most difficult and time-consuming way to

---

14. Oaks, "The Melchizedek Priesthood and the Keys," April 2020 general conference.

make decisions,[15] but such a requirement ensures that each quorum member obtains the necessary experiences and information and is able to ask the right questions before the Lord's will is manifest. President Nelson described this principal in this way:

> The calling of 15 men to the holy apostleship provides great protection for us as members of the Church. Why? Because decisions of these leaders must be unanimous. Can you imagine how the Spirit needs to move upon 15 men to bring about unanimity? These 15 men have varied educational and professional backgrounds, with differing opinions about many things. Trust me! These 15 men— prophets, seers, and revelators—know what the will of the Lord is when unanimity is reached! They are committed to see that the Lord's will truly will be done.[16]

Because of the tight controls on how and to whom general revelations is given, members of the Church everywhere can have confidence that they are from the Lord. To my knowledge, there is no other organization on earth that has similar controls in place for their organization.

FOUR DEFINING CHARACTERISTICS OF GENERAL REVELATIONS

General revelations, revelations for the entire Church and world, have certain defining characteristics that can help us know what constitute revelations from God and are binding, and distinguish them from policies, teachings, or counsel which are not—however wise and well-informed such information may be. Ignoring binding revelations does not necessarily disqualify someone from privileges within the Lord's Church, but they do disqualify them from assurances from the Holy Ghost and any attending blessings for obedience. Members

15. E. Schein, *Process Consultation Revisited*, 2nd edition (Addison Wesley Longman, 1988), 74.
16. Nelson, "Sustaining the Prophets," *Ensign*, November 2014, 74–77.

sometimes selectively choose which of the binding revelations they will accept and follow while ignoring others. Reasons are varied and nuanced; however, in my estimation it is due to competing identities that prevent them from fully considering or recognizing the primary identifiers of general revelations.

In my judgment, there are four primary identifiers of general revelations. Each identifier should command our attention and provide us with a certain ring of authenticity bearing the Lord's signature. And while it is not required that all identifiers attend every revelation in order for it to be binding upon us, they are a helpful signal to those who have ears to hear. The four identifiers are as follows:

1. The majority of the Apostles (First presidency and Quorum of the Twelve) will declare direction in writing.
2. The majority of the Apostles will sustain the direction in action.
3. The revelation's principles will be clearly identifiable in the scriptures.
4. The direction will be presented to the Church for sustaining vote to enforce the law of common consent (see D&C 28:13).

The first identifier of a general revelation was taught by Joseph Smith. Speaking on the need for the Saints to discern the truth and avoid deception, he said, "I will give you a key that will never rust,—if you will stay with the majority of the twelve apostles, and the records of the church, you will never be led astray."[17]

During the early days of the Restoration, many individuals who were called to serve in the Quorum of the Twelve apostatized, and many members followed after them. The most prominent example of the value of this teaching occurred after the martyrdom of Joseph Smith.

In a public meeting in Nauvoo, days after the prophet's death, when Sidney Rigdon, the sole survivor from the First Presidency,

---

17. *Teachings of Presidents of the Church–Joseph Smith*, 324–25. This teaching was recalled by several members who heard it taught and later recorded it.

proposed to lead the Church as its guardian, only seven of the Twelve Apostles—a bare majority—were present in Nauvoo.[18] It was that majority, led by Brigham Young, that indicated that leadership for the Church followed those who held priesthood keys and the fulness of its ordinances—keys and ordinances that were only held by them collectively. That was the only time in modern history when the "majority principle" has been needed. Ever since that time, as the Church matured, the First Presidency and Quorum of the Twelve Apostles have become more unified, fulfilling the requirement of the Lord that "every decision made by either of these quorums must be by the unanimous voice of the same; that is, every member in each quorum must be agreed to its decisions, in order to make their decisions of the same power or validity one with the other" (D&C 107:27). Every revelation in our history, even those we do not fully understand, pass this test. As Elder Neil A. Anderson has taught:

> A few question their faith when they find a statement made by a Church leader decades ago that seems incongruent with our doctrine. There is an important principle that governs the doctrine of the Church. The doctrine is taught by all 15 members of the First Presidency and Quorum of the Twelve. It is not hidden in an obscure paragraph of one talk. True principles are taught frequently and by many. Our doctrine is not difficult to find.[19]

Seeking to know the doctrine of The Church of Jesus Christ of Latter-day Saints has both longitudinal consistency among the First Presidency and Quorum of the Twelve as well as longitudinal frequency. Binding doctrines for all members are taught consistently and frequently over long periods of time.

The second identifier invites us to consider the actions of living prophets (ripples). This identifier is especially helpful when the historical record is sparse and when we are unsure if prophets have spoken

---

18. Five of the twelve were still away from Nauvoo serving missions and campaigning for Joseph Smith's candidacy for President of the United States.

19. Neil A. Anderson, "Trial of your Faith," October 2012 general conference.

prophetically. And because none of us is privy to all of the decisions and discussions of the Lord's prophets and apostles, leveraging this tool is vital.

For instance, shortly after Brigham Young and the Quorum of the Twelve Apostles had reorganized the First Presidency, Brigham Young spoke at general conference and issued a policy that restricted conferral of the priesthood upon Black members of the Church. This was a change to the policy that existed under Joseph Smith.[20] There is no written or contemporary account explaining the thinking behind the change in policy, and this has led some to conclude that Brigham Young's motivations were racially motivated. Such views are supported by later statements of President Young, statements that are clearly racist by today's standards. However, when one understands the spirit of revelation, one can watch for the collective actions of the First Presidency and Quorum of the Twelve Apostles to understand how they interpreted the change. It is their collective action in support of the change that provides the necessary evidence to members and assurance that the change in policy was the will of the Lord.[21]

Learning how apostles and prophets act in response to the revealed will of the Lord is essential to understanding why certain actions today are not taken. For example, some wonder why the prophet and other Church leaders do not offer a formal statement apologizing for the restriction of the priesthood, which for so long caused many members pain and suffering. Some critics insist that such an apology is needed despite prophets' and apostles' clear repudiation of the explanations offered by Church leaders for so many years and their

---

20. See Gospel Topics Essays, "Race and the Priesthood," churchofjesuschrist. org https://www.churchofjesuschrist.org/study/manual/gospel-topics-essays/ race-and-the-priesthood?lang=eng.

21. From 1852 until 1978, many leaders, including presidents of the Church and members of the Quorum of the Twelve, offered explanations for why the policy change was made. None of the theories advanced is accepted as doctrine for the church and binding upon members. See Gospel Topics Essays, "Race and the Priesthood." While acknowledging the mistaken explanations and reasons for the revelation, the author has found no instance of a member of the First Presidency or Quorum of the Twelve apologizing for restriction, which informs my view outlined here.

acknowledgment of the trial it was for many members. But prophets and apostles do not offer apologies for revelations from the Lord, even if the reasons for the revelations have not been provided or if the revelations themselves seem contrary to what we think is right or correct. The collective action of the First Presidency and Quorum of the Twelve on this point is evidence that the revelation was the will of the Lord and that it was the will of the Lord to have it rescinded. One need not require an apology of Church leaders to accept that the action was inspired at the time and yet be extremely grateful to God that it was repealed.[22] This, of course does, not mean that prophets and apostles will not make every attempt for reconciliation where needed. Church leaders have a long and impressive record at righting such wrongs where they exist. It does mean, however, that we can interpret their collective silence for what it was—a revelation from the Lord.

A contemporary example of watching the First Presidency and Quorum of the Twelve for the revealed will of the Lord occurred with the COVID-19 pandemic. For many members, the written and public statements to follow the direction of government and state officials in dealing with the pandemic were not enough to warrant a change in behavior (such as wearing masks). However, the collective action of the Apostles was clear. Temple worship was halted, public attendance at general conference was put on hold, and members were asked to wear masks in worship services and to social distance at other activities. These and other precautions were consistently modelled for all to see. Some will argue that the reasons leaders chose to follow this course was to avoid litigation. Or they will say that they were just trying to be good community citizens. Such reasons may be accurate. Nevertheless, they are irrelevant. Learning to recognize the collective action of the Apostles is essential. Many members missed this clear signal, however, and chose to follow voices from other sources that were rooted to competing identities.

---

22. Personally, the author finds it compelling that Brigham Young also issued the promise that at a future day all the blessings of the gospel would again be made available to Black men and women. If race was his motivation, this prophetic promise does not make any sense, as he stood to gain nothing from it at the time.

Comparing new information with what is taught in the scriptures provides us with a third assurance that what we are hearing and being asked to do is correct. Those who search the scriptures diligently hear and recognize His voice when it is spoken. "For mine elect hear my voice and harden not their hearts" (D&C 29:7).

Comparing what we hear from living prophets to the scriptures also provides us with a way of tempering ourselves. Many members become overly radicalized by prophecies of the last days and are eager to interpret their surroundings in dramatic ways. However, by searching the scriptures, we can check ourselves and place prophetic warnings into the correct context to ensure that we maintain spiritual balance. Out-of-balance members will always want to outpace prophetic cadence and march far in advance of the bands arrival. We are told to be watchful and ready, but not fanatical. The scriptures, when coupled with prophetic voice, provide the necessary counterbalances to keep us in the right way.

The fourth identifier relates to what we are asked to officially sustain through common consent. The rule of common consent was originally understood by members and leaders as a form of vote.[23] However, like many of the doctrines of the Church, it has come to mean something more nuanced as we have received more revelation on the subject. Common consent is a revealed process which provides us the privilege to sustain prophetic priorities. As such, it is not an opportunity to vote for anything. Rather, it is our opportunity to "go on-the-record" in front of God's servants for what we will accept and support. President Nelson explained: "Our sustaining of prophets is a personal commitment that we will do our utmost to uphold their prophetic priorities. Our sustaining is an oath-like indication that we recognize their calling as a prophet to be legitimate and binding upon us."[24]

When something is presented to the Church for a sustaining vote, it has always been the case that it is binding upon members. Of course, anyone can at any time elect to not follow through on what

---

23. See Gospel Topics/Common Consent, https://www.churchofjesuschrist.org/study/history/topics/common-consent?lang=eng.

24. R. Nelson, "Sustaining the Prophets," *Ensign*, November 2014, 74–77.

they indicated they would do, but that is not the point. The point is when we are presented with such occasions—and they come, at a minimum, five times per year in general, stake, and ward conferences—members need to recognize precisely what they are committing themselves to do.

Any information that carries the four identifiers outlined above should provide any member with the necessary conviction to ascend their Ladder of Inference with confidence, knowing that the information is from the Lord. The decision to do so is consistent with the child of God identity, enabling us to attribute meaning to the information as valid and true, assume that it is the Lord's will, and conclude that the correct course is to sustain it with all of our heart and mind. Furthermore, we can carry with us the assurance that eventually—as we press forward in faith, asking, seeking, and knocking—we can and will receive the understanding from the Holy Ghost that the belief we harbor is right and true. Elder David A. Bednar has taught:

> It is vitally important to always remember that the Holy Ghost will NOT prompt an individual to violate sacred covenants and disobey God's commandments. The Spirit of the Lord will NOT prompt any person to think or act in a manner that is contrary to the doctrine and the authorized practices of the Savior's restored church as contained in the Holy Scriptures, in the repeated teachings of the Lord's apostles and prophets, and in the authorized proclamations of the Council of the First Presidency and the Quorum of the Twelve Apostles.[25]

UNDERSTANDING PROPHETIC FALLIBILITY

I have noticed an increase in the discussion among members what is commonly termed "prophetic fallibility." Prophetic fallibility is the belief that because prophets are human, they make mistakes, and therefore, we must be selective and discerning of what they teach and say. Fans of prophetic fallibility point to Church leaders' incorrect

---

25. David A. Bednar, *The Spirit of Revelation*, 36.

justifications for withholding the priesthood from Black members. Additional arguments have been made about the limitations of an all-male, predominantly white leadership team. No one contests these facts. However, when one asserts that such facts constitute a mistaken course of action, one must take pause. Has the Lord ever indicated in His scriptures that we are to become skilled at discerning the truth from the error in what His prophets say? If so, I have yet to locate this doctrine. If we were to accept that idea as true, it would erode the very foundation of the Lord's Church.

The collective voice of prophets—the unanimous voice that produces general revelation for us all—is infallible and not subject to error. If it were not so, I do not know how prophetic teaching would differ at all from any other influence in the world. From the outset of the Church, prophets have dealt with the charge of human frailty as evidence of revelatory fallibility. In response to such charges, the Prophet Joseph taught, "I never told you I was perfect—but there is no error in the revelations which I have taught."[26] In other words, one should not be surprised—nor should one consider it a novelty—to learn that prophets are mortal men. With that said, *there is no error in the revelations which [they] have taught.*" The Lord has revealed that prophetic counsel is different from something that can be relied upon as error-free. It only requires that we learn to distinguish what constitutes revelation from reasons for revelations—which, as we have discussed, are very different and have different obligations for each of us. When Joseph referred to his revelations, he was referring to what I am calling general revelations for the Church, which have unique identifiers.

Our only safety in life is learning to distinguish prophetic revelations and then sustaining them fully. President Harold B. Lee, explained:

> The only safety we have as members of this church is
> to . . . learn to give heed to the words and commandments
> that the Lord shall give through His prophet. . . . There

---

26. *The Words of Joseph Smith*, ed. Andrew F. Ehat and Lyndon W. Cook (Salt Lake City: Bookcraft, 1980), 369.

will be some things that take patience and faith. You may not like what comes. . . . It may contradict your political views . . . your social views . . . interfere with . . . your social life. But if you listen to these things, as if from the mouth of the Lord Himself, . . . "the gates of hell shall not prevail against you . . . and the Lord God will disperse the powers of darkness from before you." [27]

Receiving the promised blessings for following the prophets takes patience and faith. It takes setting aside our discomfort and even anger toward what may be seen as uncomfortable teachings and sustaining those revelations fully.

Prophets have, do, and will speculate or provide reasons for the revelations they receive. However, I have observed that in this day and age, our leaders are much more cautious than their turn of the century counterparts who were more accustomed to verbal sparring over doctrinal issues as the Church struggled to establish its place in the world. Any reasons, from whatever source, which attempt to explain revelations—except those provided by the Lord—are fallible and are not binding upon us. To this point, Joseph Smith was also clear: "A prophet is only a prophet when he is acting as such." [28] This is not an excuse to selectively reject or accept what the fifteen living prophets teach, but merely a recognition that prophets are mortal and their mortality should be acknowledged.

In today's day and age, our leaders are increasingly seasoned and experienced in seeking after and recognizing the will of the Lord. We can trust that whatever we hear from them in general conference will always agree with the four identifiers and have the added witness of the Holy Ghost, the greatest personal witness of all. However, when writing books, giving interviews, or answering questions extemporaneously, their personal views may be shared. In such instances, their words do not carry the same binding effect for each of us. President Dallin H. Oaks counsels us to be cautious: "We are not bound to

---

27. *Teachings of Presidents of the Church—Harold B. Lee*, (Salt Lake City: The Church of Jesus Christ of Latter-day Saints, 2000), 84–85.
28. Joseph Smith, in *History of the Church*, 5:265.

sustain reasons for revelations, only the revelations. It is not a pattern of the Lord to give reasons. We mortals can put reasons to revelations . . . and to commandments. When we do, we're on our own. . . . The reasons tend to be man-made to a great extent. The revelations are what we sustain as the will of the Lord and that is where safety lies."[29]

PERSONAL REVELATION

In addition to the priesthood channel of revelation, we will always have our personal revelatory channel. As noted at the beginning of the chapter, it is through the personal channel by the power of the Holy Ghost that we know something is true. It is through this channel that we find guidance for our lives and for our families.[30] However, for many members of the Church, this channel of knowing is a source of frustration. Some of the frustration is due to not understanding how revelation is received. Others are frustrated because of incorrect assumptions about how the process works. As is the case for recognizing general revelations, a descent down our individual ladders is required to improve our use of the personal revelation channel.

Following prophetic direction and living day-to-day in patience and faith require acting on incomplete information, which means that leveraging the nine tools of knowing is essential. In addition to the nine tools, understanding some fundamental truths about the process of personal revelation and the underlying principles of personal revelation is also vital. Speaking about the process of personal revelation, Elder Bednar has explained, "No simple formulas or recommended action steps can guide us through this rigorous spiritual process [of revelation], . . . but 'revelation does work and in a multitude and variety of ways.'"[31] In other words, one thing we must understand about the process of personal revelation is that it is not formulaic; it is not

---

29. Dallin H. Oaks, *Life Lessons Learned* (Salt Lake City: Bookcraft, 2011), 68–69.
30. Oaks, "Two Lines of Communication," October 2010 general conference.
31. Bednar, *The Spirit of Revelation*. This book describes ten principles of revelation and scenarios to improve your ability to recognize the same in your own life. The ten principles are examples of a non-linear, non-formulaic, and illogical process.

a recipe of steps to follow to immediately get the outcome you desire. Instead, the process is non-linear, non-formulaic, and at times illogical.

PROCESS OF REVELATION: NON-LINEAR, NON-FORMULAIC, AND ILLOGICAL

A friend of mine shared with me an experience that illustrates the non-linear nature of personal revelation. He had just gotten home from work one day when his wife notified him that she had received a clear prompting to prepare dinner for a specific family in the ward. She was just finishing her preparations. My friend accompanied his wife to deliver the meal and discovered that the family was out of town. Perplexed, they prayed and felt prompted to deliver the meal to a different family, who was grateful for the meal. Afterward, his wife wondered, a bit discouraged, why she felt such clarity about a family that wasn't available to receive the meal, leading her to question her ability to receive revelation.[32] Perhaps you have had a similar experience where your inspiration did not immediately materialize in the result you expected. For me, the more people I meet, the more I hear these kinds of stories and feel certain that such experiences are more common than rare, and actually provide essential learning opportunities for our spiritual development.

Consider an experience of personal revelation from the life of Ammon recorded in the twentieth chapter of Alma in the Book of Mormon. Ammon had recently taught the son of King Lamoni and his household and had great success. Because of this success, Lamoni Jr. desires "to show Ammon to his father," Lamoni Sr. However, Ammon is prompted by the Lord that Lamoni Sr. will try to kill him, and to journey to the land of Middoni instead, where his brethren are in prison. "And the voice of the Lord came to Ammon, saying: Thou shalt not go up to the land of Nephi, for behold, the king will seek thy life; but thou shalt go to the land of Middoni; for behold, thy brother Aaron, and also Muloki and Ammah are in prison" (Alma 20:2).

---

32. Ibid., 27.

This prompting to Ammon suggests that the Lord doesn't want Ammon to do A (to not go up to the Land of Nephi because the King will seek his life), but instead do B (go to the land of Middoni and free his brethren) and that option A and B are unrelated to one another. However, Ammon came to understand that A and B were related. On his way to Middoni he encounters the very king who would have and did seek his life, and who could free his brethren from prison.

Ammon's actions are a great lesson on how to correctly act when we receive a spiritual prompting. Ammon made the will of the Lord the primary focus of his efforts (option B). When he encountered Lamoni's father on the way to Middoni, the very man the Lord indicated would seek his life (option A), he didn't question the inspiration that had led him into the exact life-threatening situation the Lord had told him to avoid. Instead, he used the inspiration he had been given and shared his purpose with Lamoni Sr. As it turned out, it was these words that first impacted Lamoni's father's heart (see Alma 20:24). The Lord knew what words would impact Lamoni Sr. the most, and he revealed them to Ammon (option B). The Lord intended to free Ammon's brethren, but he also had his eye on Lamoni Sr.

What does this account teach us about the non-linear nature of personal revelation? We may receive a clear answer to do something (option B) and make an incorrect assumption about why the Lord gave us this message. However, as we act in faith in response to what was given, He will, in the end, reveal His ultimate purpose or the object of His intention (option A) "which are expedient for us" (1 Nephi 17:30). As the scriptures teach, this added revelation happens "line upon line; here a little, and there a little" (Isaiah 28:10). Learning to act upon feelings that "we feel are right" (D&C 9:8) is vital to the revelatory process.[33]

Why doesn't the Lord just reveal option A from the outset? Wouldn't it make more sense to just give someone the answer they want when they ask? Why not just give people what they want when they want it? Ultimately, the reasons God proceeds with us as He does

---

33. Oaks, *Life Lessons Learned*, 77.

are known only to Him.[34] Still, some reasons seem apparent in His dealings with each of us. Let's consider a few of them.

First, it seems clear that the revelatory process must be non-linear to account for the choices of all of His sons and daughters. This means that His interventions are timed so that they come at the right time, at the right place. It also implies that some circuitous and unsolicited answers will be needed. Speaking of unsolicited spiritual impressions, Elder Richard G. Scott taught that the Holy Ghost will honor the agency of those He prompts:

> Impressions of the Spirit can come in response to urgent prayer or unsolicited when needed. Sometimes the Lord reveals truth to you when you are not actively seeking it, such as when you are in danger and do not know it. However, the Lord will not force you to learn. You must exercise your agency to authorize the Spirit to teach you. As you make this a practice in your life, you will be more perceptive to the feelings that come with spiritual guidance. Then, when that guidance comes, sometimes when you least expect it, you will recognize it more easily.[35]

The non-linear nature of personal revelation is the fact that it is also non-formulaic. This means that it is not something that can be automated through a series of steps, but instead can be encouraged by adhering to principles aligned with righteousness. This approach requires the individual to learn in order to obtain revelations. Elder Dale G. Renlund taught that the purpose of mortality "is not for us to do what is right; rather, it is [to learn] to choose to do what

---

34. "The Still and Small Principle," Elder Bednar explained, "even as we strive to be faithful and obedient, there are simply times when the direction, assurance, and peace of the Spirit are not readily recognizable in our lives. . . . Why would the Lord not make the voice of the Spirit easy to recognize all the time? I would suggest a simple answer—because God trusts us and wants us to grow" (Ibid., 11).

35. Richard G. Scott, "To Acquire Spiritual Guidance," October 2009 general conference.

is right."[36] Our individual learning is paramount to our purpose on earth. Consequently, the Lord has arranged our time in our second estate to accommodate our individual learning needs. President Nelson has recently emphasized the gradual, process of learning to recognize the Lord's will through personal revelation: "Pray in the name of Jesus Christ about your concerns, your fears, your weaknesses—yes, the very longings of your heart. And then listen! Write the thoughts that come to your mind. Record your feelings and follow through with actions that you are prompted to take. As you repeat this process day after day, month after month, year after year, you will "grow into the principle of revelation."[37]

In addition to being non-formulaic and orientated towards learning, personal revelation is often illogical, with information given according to God's infinite foreknowledge. Sometimes God directs us to act in ways that fulfill His purposes, though He may not reveal to us how this is so—at least immediately. We see this principle in play in the life of Nephi and Mormon in making the small plates. In 1 Nephi 19:2–4, Nephi explains:

> And I knew not at the time when I made them [large plates] that I should be commanded of the Lord to make these plates [small plates. . . . And after I had made these plates [small plates] by way of commandment, I, Nephi, received a commandment that the ministry and the prophecies, the more plain and precious parts of them, should be written upon these plates [small plates]; and that the things which were written should be kept for the instruction of my people, who should possess the land, and also for otherwise purposes, which purposes are known unto the Lord. Wherefore, I, Nephi, did make a record upon the other plates [large plates], which gives an account, or which gives a greater account of the wars and contentions and destructions of my people. And this have I done, and commanded my people what they should do

---

36. Dale G. Renlund, "Choose You This Day," *Ensign*, October 2018.
37. Russell M. Nelson, "Revelation for the Church, Revelation for our Lives," *Ensign*, April 2018.

after I was gone; and that these plates [small plates] should be handed down from one generation to another, or from one prophet to another, until further commandments of the Lord.

Notice that Nephi was first commanded to make another set of plates before He knew what he was supposed to engrave on them, and that he was to ensure future generations engraved similar content on them "until further commandments of the Lord" would come. He also indicates that he didn't know what the plates would be used for, only that they were "for otherwise purposes, which purposes are known unto the Lord." Approximately nine hundred years later, Mormon would find the small plates and be similarly prompted to include them in his record without knowing why, only that "they are pleasing unto the Lord and will be pleasing unto his brethren" at a future day (Words of Mormon 1:3–7). For all that was revealed to Nephi and Mormon of the coming forth of their records in the last day to their seed, they do not appear to have known that a primary purpose for the small plates would be to replace lost content from the Book of Lehi—an event that did not occur until 1828 (see D&C 10). For each of them, the prompting must have seemed, at a minimum, illogical.

Personally, I have seen the non-linear, non-formulaic, and illogical elements of personal revelation displayed as I have extended callings to members to serve others in their ward or stake. Sometimes, we will feel clear inspiration to extend callings to ward members who do not accept them (illogical). On these occasions, I have wondered why I would feel strongly about something that did not occur. At other times, I have felt inspired to extend callings to serve but the member's service led to hard feelings among other ward members or perhaps to trials of faith for others in their path (non-linear). Similar experiences may have happened to you. In such instances, you may have wondered whether you or others correctly interpreted the inspiration that was given.

Over time, I have come to trust that the main issue has to do with my own expectations—what I think should happen. In each case, these expectations were based on incorrect assumptions. Perhaps I had witnessed one person accept and grow in a calling, and I assumed the blessing would unfold in the same way for someone else. However, as it was with Nephi and Mormon, so it is with each of us. The Lord's purposes are not always made known. All He requires of you and me is to act and trust that His purposes are in motion: "For my thoughts are not your thoughts, neither are your ways my ways, saith the Lord. For as the heavens are higher than the earth, so are my ways higher than your ways, and my thoughts than your thoughts (Isaiah 55:8–9).

He knows the destinies of all nations and sees the end from the beginning. His purposes to redeem all of His spirit children will not be frustrated. Thus, the what, how, when, and why of revelation will always work toward His ultimate objectives.

Another instance from the scriptures where we see these principles in action occurs during the preaching of Aaron and his companions in Alma 21:1–16. In verses 1–15, Mormon summarizes a variety of places Aaron and his companions taught the word among the Amalekites, none of which were successful and nearly all of which brought failure and personal suffering. In verses 16-17, Mormon explains,

> And they went forth whithersoever they were led by the Spirit of the Lord, preaching the word of God in every synagogue of the Amalekites, or in every assembly of the Lamanites where they could be admitted. And it came to pass that the Lord began to bless them, insomuch that they brought many to the knowledge of the truth; yea, they did convince many of their sins, and of the traditions of their fathers, which were not correct.

Note that Aaron and his companions were being led everywhere by the Spirit. The Spirit was leading them into situations where success was not immediate and where suffering occurred (illogical). Why? Ultimately, and for reasons known only to God, "they did convince many of their sins and of the traditions of their fathers which were not correct."

Sometimes our guidance directs us to someone actively seeking help. At other times, however, our efforts fulfill other purposes, and our path is less straightforward than we might hope. What is clear is that as we act in faith, we can know we are on God's errand and that ultimately His purposes will be fulfilled. This helps when, like Aaron and his comrades, suffering precedes our success.

Only the Savior knows the pleading and seeking of every human heart and mind. Only He hears the soul-cry of all who anguish and call out for help in the dark of night. Thus, the revelatory process must account for the faith of His children in the moment it is needed, and not before. God knows who can endure a period of seeming unresponsiveness and still carry on with limited information, and He knows those whose faith is fragile and who need more immediate reassurance. For all of His billions and billions of spirit children, God manages the timing and method of revelatory-delivery on schedule and perfectly situated.

One thing that has become clear to me is that adopting the child of God identity is essential to increasing our ability to understand the Lord's purposes in His revelations to each of us. Acquiring the child of God identity requires that we learn to surrender the expected sequence and timing of events in our lives, expectations that are often linked to other competing identities. We must learn to discern— and come to anticipate and know—"the dealings of that God who has created us" (1 Nephi 2:12), as we trust in God's character and love for us. Sister Michelle Craig explained Nephi's familiar phrase in (1 Nephi 3:7) of the Lord "preparing a way for us to accomplish the thing which He hath commanded" as follows: "Note that Nephi says, '*a* way'—not '*the* way.'" Do we miss or dismiss personal errands from the Lord because He has prepared 'a way' different from the one we expect? . . . Trust God to lead you, even if that way looks different than you expected or is different from others."[38]

Elder Jeffrey R. Holland once shared an experience he had with his son that helps illustrate this point.[39] He described a situation where as he and his son were traveling home they arrived at a fork in the road. For a moment, they wondered which way they should go. Eventually they prayed to know which was right and felt good about taking the road on the right. They travelled a short distance down the road and soon it was a dead end. So, they turned around and drove back to the fork and proceeded down the left path.

---

38. Michelle D. Craig, "Spiritual Capacity," *Ensign*, October 2019.
39. See video "Wrong Roads," churchofjesuschrist.org.

After a short time, Elder Holland's son asked his father why they had felt good about going down a road that was the wrong road. Elder Holland explained that in this instance, the best way to provide the knowledge to them that they were indeed on the correct path was to show them the wrong path.

Sometimes, we will be required to trust feelings that in the short run appear incorrect, as we learn to discern "the dealings of that God who created us" (1 Nephi 2:12). In short, we must be willing to sacrifice our own expectations and preferences to God and trust in the promptings and inspiration that comes. Elder Neal A. Maxwell taught faith in God requires 1) trusting in God's will; 2) *His way of doing things*; and 3) trust in his timing.[40] Elder Oaks has noted that doing the right thing at the wrong time can leave one confused.[41] This includes doing the right thing, at the right time, but failing to understand His way of doing things. If we take the time to ponder upon the Lord's dealings with His children, we will, like Elder Holland and his son, *come to see* the Lord tutoring us in a loving way that we can trust, and which will build our faith and reliance upon Him.

Continually learning the spirit of revelation makes us more likely to accept prophetic counsel with patience and faith. Knowing the difference between revelations we must follow and opinions that do not require our adherence is essential. Becoming more discerning and willing followers of the Lord's words prepares us to consider a fundamental and essential truth taught by prophets from the beginning, namely, we must repent.

---

40. Neal A. Maxwell, *Even as I Am* (Salt Lake City: Bookcraft, 1982), 93.
41. Oaks, *Life Lessons Learned* (Salt Lake City: Deseret Book, 2011), 120.

CHAPTER 5

Changing Our Mind and Heart

Helaman 15:7

At the center of a changed heart, one that turns away from competing identities and fully embraces the child of God identity, is a love for repentance. Repentance is essential and fundamental to becoming the person God wants us to become. It is one of the first principles of the gospel because it reflects the primary mindset of one desiring to be transformed in and through the Atonement of Jesus Christ.

At the heart of repentance is a feeling that we have done wrong, violating the light of Christ within us. This feeling is described in the scriptures by various words: sorrow, anguish, torment, and remorse. Remorse is used in the scriptures three times and always by Alma the Younger (see Alma 5:18; 29:5; 42:18), presumably because he was poignantly brought to feel the effects of his actions in an acute and dramatic way (see Mosiah 27 and Alma 36).

Alma's description of remorse is similar to what psychotherapists, management theorists, and philosophers describe as regret. Studies on regret have concluded that regret is an integral part of being human and is beneficial to living a happy life. Regret is a universal emotion. In studies on commonly felt emotions, people mention regret the most second only to love.[1] All human beings, as it turns out, are hardwired

---

1. S. Shimanoff, "Commonly named emotions in everyday conversations," *Perceptual and Motor Skills*, 1984.

to feel regret, the exceptions being children,[2] and individuals suffering from developmental, degenerative, or traumatic brain injuries.

Regret is essential to changing our heart and mind and initiating the repentance process. Daniel Pink, in his book *The Power of Regret*, noted: "Regret is not dangerous or abnormal, a deviation from the steady path to happiness. It is healthy and universal, an integral part of being human. Regret is also valuable. It clarifies. It instructs. Done right, it needn't drag us down; it can lift us up."[3]

Regret is best understood not as a thing but as a process. The process is facilitated by our ability—and frequent tendency—to travel backward in time in our minds and rewrite our capabilities. As we visit our past experiences, we make comparisons between what is and what might have been and then assess blame to ourselves for the action or inaction taken. Our ability to assume responsibility for our actions lies at the core of our ability to feel regret.

Remembering and feeling regret is beneficial so long as we do not linger upon our actions for too long. Lingering upon our regrets or re-playing our failures repeatedly in our mind brings debilitating effects. Studies show that people who ruminate over and replay their regrets frequently are more likely to report life dissatisfaction and difficulty coping with negative life events,[4] as well as other physical and mental health ailments.[5] Another common problem with regret, according to one author, occurs "when we frame regret as a judgement of our

---

2. Interestingly, children develop the ability to experience regret as early as age six and anticipate regret by age eight. Age eight is the age designated by the Lord when individuals become accountable before Him (see D&C 18:42; 20:71; and 68:25) and capable of repentance. The ability to feel and anticipate the emotion of regret is essential to repentance. See R. Guttentag and J. Ferrell, "Reality compared with its alternatives: Age differences in judgements of regret and relief" (*Developmental Psychology* 40, no. 5, 2004, 764. See also B. Uprichard and T. McCormick, "Becoming kinder: Prosocial choice and the development of interpersonal regret," *Child Development* 90, no. 4, 2019, 486–504).

3. D. Pink, *The Power of Regret* (Penguin Books, 2002), 8.

4. C. Saffrey, A. Summerville, and N. Roese, "Praise for regret: People value regret above other negative motions," *Motivation and Emotion* 32, no. 1, 2008, 46–54.

5. M. Monroe, J. Skowronski, W. MacDonald, and S. Wood, "The mildly depressed experience more post-decisional regret than the non-depressed," *Journal of Social and Clinical Psychology* 24, no. 5, 2005, 665–90.

underlying character—who we are—instead of an assessment of our taken action/inaction in a particular situation—what we did."[6] When dealt with in this way, regret serves its purpose and can help make us wise. Regret is for helping us learn from past mistakes to guide our decisions toward what we inherently know is right and good.

Regret brings many benefits when applied properly. In fact, three primary benefits of regret have been shown by research, including improved decision-making, elevated performance, and strengthened sense of meaning and connectedness.[7] The key for each of us is to use the discomforting feelings of regret to reflect upon our actions/inactions that were incorrect, exercise faith in Jesus Christ, turn away from our past decisions that violated His commandments, and turn toward His standard of righteousness. In short, we must use regret to repent.

Nephi famously taught that it is through Jesus's "grace we are saved, after all we can do" (2 Nephi 25:23). I believe most of us read this scripture and believe "all we can do" refers to our efforts to live obediently as we continuously exercise faith in Christ. This is probably true; however, I wonder if "all we can do" is even more precise than we think in what is required of us. One other time in the standard works—one time—the same phrase is used, but it is used very specifically about "all that we can do." It occurs in Alma 24:11 and 15 and is spoken by King Anti-Nephi-Lehi in reference to what he and his people did to receive Christ's forgiveness. Simply put, all they could do was to repent. "It was all we could do," he said, "to repent sufficiently before God that he would take away our stain" (Alma 24:11). Perhaps repentance really is the only thing we can do—the only thing He requires of each of us—because it is the only thing that provides an opportunity for us to use our agency to "offer our whole souls as an offering unto him" (Omni 1:26) and be saved. It is only through repentance that we lay our will upon His altar as an offering to be consumed.

---

6. *Power of Regret*, 54.
7. B. Ford, P. Lam, O. John, and I. Mauss, "The psychological health benefits of accepting negative emotions and thoughts: laboratory, diary, and longitudinal evidence," *Journal of Personality and Social Psychology* 115, no. 6, 2018, 1075.

To more fully repent, it is necessary to understand and accept some basic truths about God and His plan for each of us. Getting the basics right allows us to repent and—like Moses—learn things we "never had supposed" (Moses 1:10).

God is our Father. We are His sons and daughters. We are accountable to Him for the lives that we live and will be judged by Him for our actions. He has affixed a punishment for violating eternal laws, but he has revealed what is right that we might avoid suffering eternal punishment. Violation of divine law—or sin—makes our spirits unclean and unfit to live with a pure and holy God. Justice requires that each of us provide restitution to God for our sins in order to avoid eternal punishment. However, as sinners, we are helpless to offer restitution and so fully deserving of justice. God sent His Son—Jesus Christ—to pay our debts to justice and settle our accounts. Because He paid our debts, He is our creditor and sets the terms of our redemption. His terms are His gospel. If we exercise faith in Him and repent of our sins, He promises that He will advocate our cause at the day of judgment. If, on the other hand, we reject Him and His terms, we will be exposed to the demands of justice, which will fill us with torment, regret, and remorse of conscience (see Alma 5:18). These are the fundamentals.

What we decide about Jesus and His gospel is critical because—as mentioned—we are accountable to God for how we use our time on earth. Thus, God commanded Joseph Smith at the outset of the Restoration, "Say nothing but repentance unto this generation,"[8] indicating it is "the thing that would be of the most worth unto [us] . . . to bring souls unto [Him]."[9] Repentance is, therefore, not an optional function of salvation but a requirement to enter into God's presence—as the Savior explained to the Nephites: "Now this is the commandment, repent all ye ends of the earth and come unto me and be baptized in my name that ye may sanctified by the reception of the Holy Ghost, that ye may stand spotless before me at the last day."[10]

---

8. D&C 6:9, 11:9.
9. D&C 15:6.
10. 3 Nephi 27:20.

Because the scriptures emphasize our need to be cleansed from sin to enter God's presence, it is easy to associate repentance with something undesirable. However, that is not how the Lord sees it and not what Latter-day prophets have taught about it. Repentance is a gift that opens the doors to the Lord's blessings in our lives. For instance, the scriptures teach that through repentance, the guilt we feel when we commit sin "can be swept away."[11] We can be "filled with joy," "receive a remission of our sins," and ultimately experience a "peace of conscience."[12] Additionally, we can be filled with the marvelous light of God and be "pained no more."[13] In short, repentance invites us to feel the peace that flows from Jesus Christ.[14]

Perhaps the greatest gift we exercise as we repent is our gift of agency.[15] Repentance is the path offered to us from a loving Savior who offers us mercy while still honoring our divine gift of moral agency. It remains within each of us to "choose liberty and eternal life through the great Mediator of all men, or to choose captivity and death, according to the captivity and power of the devil."[16] How we use our agency here and now, when it really matters, will make all the difference then, in a future day, when options are limited for the unrepentant—when "the rebellious are pierced with much sorrow, when

---

11. Enos 1:6.

12. Mosiah 4:3.

13. Mosiah 27:29.

14. "Peace is the precious fruit of a righteous life. It is possible because of the Atonement of the Savior. It is earned through full repentance, for that leads to refreshing forgiveness. Repentance opens the doors of enlightenment and aids inspiration" (R. Scott, "The Path to Peace and Joy," October 2000 general conference).

15. "Christ died not to save indiscriminately but to offer repentance. We rely "wholly upon the merits of him who is mighty to save" in the process of repentance, but acting to repent is a self-willed change. So by making repentance a condition for receiving the gift of grace, God enables us to retain responsibility for ourselves. Repentance respects and sustains our moral agency" (D. Christofferson, "Free Forever to Act for Themselves," October 2014 general conference).

16. 2 Nephi 2:27.

their iniquities shall be spoken upon the housetops, and their secret acts revealed."[17]

Repentance requires change, and nothing but a total change will do. President Nelson recently testified, "When we choose to repent, we choose to change! We allow the Savior to transform us into the best version of ourselves. We choose to grow spiritually and receive joy—the joy of redemption in Him. When we choose to repent, we choose to become more like Jesus Christ!"[18]

The requirement of change is not easy. It can include surrendering parts of our identity, including beliefs and attitudes acquired through our families or environment from birth. Elder Dallin H. Oaks explained: "The gospel of Jesus Christ challenges us to change. 'Repent' is its most frequent message, and repenting means giving up all of our practices—personal, family, ethnic, and national—that are contrary to the commandments of God."[19]

The Book of Mormon tells of a people who changed in this way. The Anti-Nephi-Lehis did "all that they could do to repent of all their sins" and were "convinced of the traditions of their wicked fathers," such that they did "hide away their swords . . . yea, even did bury them deep in the earth" as a testimony to God "that rather than shed the blood of their brethren they would give up their own lives; and rather than take away from a brother they would give unto him; and rather than spend their days in idleness they would labor abundantly with their own hands."[20] Their commitment to change involved laying down traditions and beliefs that justified killing, stealing, and idleness—beliefs that had been taught to them by their fathers for generations as the correct way to think and act.

---

17. D&C 1:3; see also Alma 34:34: "Ye cannot say, when ye are brought to that awful crisis, that I will repent, that I will return to my God. Nay, ye cannot say this; for that same spirit which doth possess your bodies at the time that ye go out of this life, that same spirit will have power to possess your body in that eternal world."

18. Rusell M. Nelson, "We Can Do Better and Be Better," October 2019 general conference.

19. Dallin H. Oaks, "Repentance and Change," October 2003 general conference.

20. See Alma 24:6–19.

However widespread our change of mind and complete our behavioral adjustments, repentance is incomplete unless it is centered in Jesus Christ. "Real repentance," taught Elder Renlund, "must involve faith in the Lord Jesus Christ, faith that He can change us, faith that He can forgive us, and faith that He will help us avoid more mistakes."[21] When we violate eternal laws, we receive eternal consequences, unless we access the power of the Mediator and apply His atoning blood on our behalf. We access His power by exercising faith in Him, repenting of our sins, and keeping His commandments, which are the greatest expression of His love to us.

The Atonement of Jesus Christ can heal all wounds. The scriptures are clear about this fact. "The Atonement can reclaim each one of us, [and] bears no scars," testified Elder Packer. "It can wash clean every stain no matter how difficult or how long or how many times repeated."[22] Additionally, the Atonement of Jesus Christ is applied immediately, at the first intimation of our repentance—at the commencement of changing our heart and mind. Consider these scriptures:

- "If ye will repent and harden not your hearts, immediately shall the great plan of redemption be brought about unto you."[23]
- "Yea, and as often as my people repent will I forgive them their trespasses against me."[24]
- "But as oft as they repented and sought forgiveness, with real intent, they were forgiven."[25]

When we repent, the plan of mercy begins to work on our behalf.[26] It is for this reason, regarding our sins, that we should—as Alma instructed his son Corianton—"not endeavor to excuse ourselves in the least point."[27]

---

21. Dale G. Renlund, "Repentance: A Joyful Choice," October 2016 general conference.
22. Boyd K. Packer, "The Plan of Happiness," April 2015 general conference.
23. Alma 34:31.
24. Mosiah 26:30.
25. Moroni 6:8.
26. "According to justice, the plan of redemption could not be brought about, only on conditions of repentance" (Alma 42:13).
27. Alma 42:30.

"Excusing ourselves" is an activity of the mind and part of what makes repentance so difficult. Changing our minds means deciding that God's view of what constitutes sin matters more than our own. Elder Renlund recently taught that five attitudes affect our ability to change our minds: 1) blaming others; 2) minimizing our mistakes; 3) thinking God's love supersedes His commandments; 4) separating God from His commandments; and 5) misunderstanding the doctrine of repentance.[28] Do we have any such beliefs? Are there conditions in our lives for which we harbor blame? Which of our actions do we minimize? Do we believe that God's love for us—though absolute—will prevent divine justice from its claim upon us if we have not repented? Do we tell ourselves that in our case, repentance is not needed? If so, we must repent and not "excuse ourselves" any longer.

The passing of time does not forgive sin; only the Savior can do that. We may put our sins from our mind. The impact of our deeds may fade away. Yet their effects remain, imprinted on our spirit to be recalled clearly and completely, unless finally resolved. And if left unresolved—in the day of judgment—our souls will be awakened to their presence, and we will see them distinctly, including their effects upon others.[29]

"When Jesus asks you and me to 'repent,'" taught President Nelson, "He is inviting us to change our mind, our knowledge, our spirit—even the way we breathe. He is asking us to change the way we love, think, serve, spend our time, treat our wives, teach our children, and even care for our bodies. Nothing is more liberating, more ennobling, or more crucial to our individual progression than is a regular, daily focus on repentance."[30]

Yet, as we strive to repent, we are liable to tell ourselves stories that are not true. These stories may be of our own making, environmentally fostered, or come from the adversary, but they are not from God. On this point, Latter-day prophets are clear. Said President Nelson: "Too many people consider repentance as punishment—something

---

28. Renlund, "Repentance: A Joyful Choice," October 2016 general conference.
29. See Mosiah 2:38–39. See also, Elder Neil Anderson, "Repent that I May Heal You," October 2009 general conference.
30. Nelson, "We Can Do Better and Be Better."

to be avoided except in the most serious circumstances. But this feeling of being penalized is engendered by Satan. He tries to block us from looking to Jesus Christ, who stands with open arms, hoping and willing to heal, forgive, cleanse, strengthen, purify, and sanctify us."[31]

Repentance is not a punishment for sin. It is our escape from an eventual punishment at the day of judgment.

Another story we tell ourselves is that because of our sins, our course is set and we are without hope of forgiveness or redemption. This also is not true. Elder Packer taught: "The angels of the devil convince some that they are born to a life from which they cannot escape and are compelled to live in sin. The most wicked of lies is that they cannot change and repent and that they will not be forgiven. That cannot be true. . . . Christ is the Creator, the Healer. What He made, He can fix."[32]

Some of our thoughts are retained as we repent and continue with us long afterward. Such thoughts can have a way of tormenting us, filling us with sudden, shameful chills of memory. Even in this there is divine purpose. Elder Neil A. Anderson explained it this way: "Sometimes we wonder why we remember our sins long after we have forsaken them. . . . The Lord at times allows the residue of our mistakes to rest in our memory. It is a vital part of our mortal learning. As we honestly confess our sins, restore what we can to the offended, and forsake our sins by keeping the commandments, we are in the process of receiving forgiveness."[33]

In the divine ecology of souls, it appears even the memories of misdeeds have a leavening effect upon us, drawing us closer to our Savior and fostering gratitude for His abundant mercy toward us.

Once we muster the faith to change the way we think, we are positioned to change the way we act. Changing our behavior to align with God's commandments can be painful. As with changing our minds, changing our actions must be done with what the scriptures

31. Nelson, "We Can Do Better and Be Better."
32. Packer, "I Will Remember Your Sins No More," April 2006 general conference. See also 2 Nephi 1:13; 9:45; Jacob 3:11; Alma 26:13–14; and Moroni 7:17–19.
33. Neil A. Anderson, "Repent that I May Heal You," October 2009 general conference.

call "a broken heart and contrite spirit" and "real intent." These factors are the evidence of our desire to change, and it is upon these factors—and these alone—that the Savior fills us with the sanctifying power of his spirit. "Wherefore, redemption cometh in and through the holy Messiah, for he is full of grace and truth. Behold, he offereth himself a sacrifice for sin, to answer the ends of the law, unto all those who have a broken heart and a contrite spirit, and unto none else can the ends of the law be answered."[34]

Genuine repentance requires that we feel remorse for our actions—remorse born from recognition that our actions have offended, and perhaps harmed, our fellowmen and the God we love.[35]

Striving to change our behavior requires more of us than just abandoning past deeds. It also requires that we confess our sins to God and to those who may have been harmed, and that we make restitution by whatever means necessary.[36] For more serious sins, we must confess to those who hold priesthood keys—to the bishop, in most cases, or the stake president. In such cases, restrictions may be imposed on certain privileges within the Lord's Church. The restrictions are meant to help us as we align our behavior to the Lord's commandments. They will also protect us from partaking of spiritual things unworthily, increase our desire to participate in them commendably. One of the greatest blessings of repentance occurs when an individual again partakes of sacred ordinances with the knowledge that he or she has been forgiven by the Lord.

Repentance is not an event that we pull out for significant moments in our life—like Christmas china—only to be stored away again after things settle down. Instead, it is a process that requires agency, striving, and time to do its work. President Nelson has taught: "Repentance is not an event; it is a process. It is the key to happiness

---

34. 2 Nephi 2:6–7. See also 2 Corinthians 7:10 for the requirement of godly sorrow to accompany sincere repentance.

35. Elder M. Russell Ballard has taught: "For those who have strayed, the Savior has provided a way back. But it is not without pain. Repentance is not easy; it takes time—painful time!" (Keeping Covenants, *Ensign*, May 1993, 7).

36. D&C 58:42–43: "Behold, he who has repented of his sins, the same is forgiven, and I, the Lord, remember them no more. By this ye may know if a man repenteth of his sins—behold, he will confess them and forsake them."

and peace of mind. When coupled with faith, repentance opens our access to the power of the Atonement of Jesus Christ."[37]

The process of repentance is most often non-linear, meaning that our ability to shed former beliefs and implement new behaviors does not happen all at once. Nor is the improvement constant. This can be discouraging and lead us to engender more thoughts that we should not accept as true. The Lord knows that our ascent to become Latter-day Saints in thought, word, and deed would not be easy, nor automatic, so we should follow His lead and be patient in the process of change. Of this point Elder Anderson taught: "Sometimes in our repentance, in our daily efforts to become more Christlike, we find ourselves repeatedly struggling with the same difficulties. . . . Don't be discouraged. If you are striving and working to repent, you are in the process of repenting."[38]

Repentance is about learning and growing. Elder Lynn G. Robbins, then of the Presidency of the Seventy, described "repentance [as] God's ever-accessible gift that allows and enables us to go from failure to failure without any loss of enthusiasm. Repentance isn't His backup plan in the event we might fail. Repentance *is* His plan, knowing that we will."[39]

How do we know the actions or thoughts we should repent of? Here are a few suggestions: First, we know we need to repent if any of our conduct is not aligned with the Lord's commandments. His commandments constitute behavioral guardrails to keep us within the bounds He has set.[40] Second, we know what to repent of by

---

37. Nelson, "We Can Do Better and Be Better." See also, Anderson, "Repent that I May Heal You": "For most, repentance is more a journey than a one-time event. It is not easy. To change is difficult. It requires running into the wind, swimming upstream. Jesus said, 'If any man will come after me, let him deny himself, and take up his cross and follow me.' Repentance is turning away from some things, such as dishonesty, pride, anger, and impure thoughts, and turning toward other things, such as kindness, unselfishness, patience, and spirituality. It is 're-turning' toward God."

38. Ibid., 2009. See also Lynn Robbins, "Until Seventy Times Seven," April 2018 general conference.

39. Lynn G. Robbins, "Until Seventy Times Seven."

40. D&C 82:8–9.

asking God through prayer.[41] "And all things whatsoever ye shall ask in prayer, believing, ye shall receive."[42] Third, we hearken to the words of our living prophet, who identified three areas where repentance may be needed: 1) how we care for our bodies; 2) how we treat our spouse; and 3) how we place the welfare of others ahead of our own.[43] Fourth, we can remember times in our lives when we felt darkened because of something we did or said.[44] To a group of elders assembled in Kirtland, the Lord taught, "Your minds in times past have been darkened because of unbelief and because you have treated lightly the things you have received."[45] When we ignore or disobey commandments from God, the light of the Holy Ghost withdraws from us and it is replaced by the shadow of sin.

The good news of the gospel is that we have been redeemed by a long-suffering and merciful Savior who knows our struggles and desires us to be better. Thankfully, He understands perfectly that we "are prone to wander from the God we love,"[46] and He stretches out His mighty arm to save us anyway. Elder Richard G. Scott testified: "The joyful news for anyone who desires to be rid of the consequences of past poor choices is that the Lord sees weaknesses differently than He does rebellion. Whereas the Lord warns that unrepented rebellion will bring punishment, when the Lord speaks of weaknesses, it is always with mercy."[47]

This brings us back to merciful Jesus. What can our merciful Savior teach us about repentance? Jesus Christ aced His mortal exam. He did not miss a single question, and He filled out the extra credit questions for good measure. But oh, how it tested Him! Never was a test so laden with difficulty and so extreme—difficulty that caused

---

41. Anderson, "Repent that I May Heal You."
42. Matthew 21:22.
43. Nelson, "We Can Do Better and Be Better."
44. D&C 10:2. On two separate occasions, the Lord taught Joseph Smith about the darkness that comes to one's mind when they ignore commandments or disobey them.
45. D&C 84:54.
46. Chris Rice, "Come Thou Font of Every Blessing," verse 8.
47. Richard G. Scott, "Personal Strength through the Atonement of Jesus Christ," *Ensign,* November 2013, 83.

Him to stumble, fall to the ground, and plead for relief. By assuming the burden of our infirmities and sin, He has set the testing requirements for each of us, and He is on our side. He allows us seemingly endless chances—seventy times seven—to place our faith in Him, repent, and improve. Our success is His success—because, as he said to Moses, "This is my work and my glory to bring to pass the immortality and eternal life of man" (Moses 1:39).[48] Or as He said to the Prophet Joseph, "Remember the worth of souls is great in the sight of God. For, behold, the Lord your Redeemer suffered death in the flesh; wherefore he suffered the pain of all men, *that all men might repent and come unto him*"[49]

By embracing repentance, we make it possible to more fully incorporate the child of God identity, aligning ourselves to receive truth. Meanwhile, we avoid setting up stakes that might keep us from a fullness of truth. Additionally, repentance keeps our hearts supple and receptive to the Lord's guiding influence, even the influence of His Spirit, which is rapidly becoming an imperative for latter-day survival. As President Nelson testified, "In coming days, it will not be possible to survive spiritually without the guiding, directing, comforting, and constant influence of the Holy Ghost."[50]

---

48. Robbins, "Until Seventy Times Seven."
49. D&C 18:10–11; emphasis added.
50. Nelson, "Revelation for the Church, Revelation for our Lives," *Ensign*, April 2018, 96.

CHAPTER 6

All Things in Commotion

D&C 88:91

Now that we have introduced all of the tools to fully embrace our child of God identity and live with patience and faith, the next step is to gain some experience applying them. Using Figure 17 from chapter 3 as a guide, I have selected certain issues for further consideration. Again, as stated at the outset, it is not the goal of this work to tell anyone how or what they should believe. Instead, its aims are to introduce tools and concepts to help us live "with patience and faith" and to encourage us to consider the effects of our individual identity upon our choices. We will use some of the biggest obstacles facing members of The Church of Jesus Christ of Latter-day Saints as case studies to apply the tools. The reader is invited to consider the facts for each issue and apply the tools discussed.

This section considers a few of the largest circles from Figure 17, namely, "Incredulity over Church History." Because Church members debate so many separate issues related to Church history, I have selected a few that seem to gain the most publicity online and on social media. The issue and supporting information—in other words, the data pool—are provided on the left side of the page. The second half of each topic is divided into three separate sections for exploring thoughts and ideas that could help you apply the tools discussed in this work. After considering the information in the case, readers are invited to apply the tools and generate additional questions and information needed to satisfy their minds for each issue.

RACE AND THE PRIESTHOOD[1]

Facts and Information

- Joseph Smith knowingly conferred the priesthood upon a few Black members of the Church during his lifetime.
- No doctrine revealed through Joseph Smith implies any limitation of priesthood conferral except worthiness.
- The first statement of priesthood restriction was based on lineage, from Brigham Young in 1849.[2]
- In 1852 Brigham Young first announced a policy restricting the conferral of priesthood authority upon black men and participation in temple ordinances by men and women.
- In 1852, Brigham Young indicated at a future date (millennium) the restriction would be removed; the future timing softened over time.[3]
- The change of policy by Brigham Young was the only major policy deviation from the foundation left by Joseph Smith.
- After the change in policy, tradition, common Christian beliefs, and certain scriptural interpretations shaped Church leaders' perceptions for the reasons for the ban.[4]
- Brigham Young and other Church leaders suggested lineage and premortal unfaithfulness as reasons for withholding the priesthood.
- Though widely accepted by members, no historical explanation was required for members to believe and remain in good standing.[5]

---

1. See Gospel Topic Essays, "Race and the Priesthood," https://www. churchofjesuschrist.org/study/manual/gospel-topics-essays/race-and-the-priesthood?lang=eng.
2. *Journal History of the Church*, February 13, 1849, Church History Library; microfilm copy in Harold B. Lee Library, Brigham Young University, Provo, Utah. See *Journal History of the Church*, June 2, 1847, "William Appleby to Brigham Young, raising the question."
3. E. Kimball, "Spencer W. Kimball and the Revelation on Priesthood," *BYU Studies Quarterly*. Vol. 47, Iss. 2, 2008, 10.
4. Ibid., 1.
5. Ibid., 8–9, footnote 8.

- Members were required to sustain the restriction as the will of the Lord.
- No scriptural basis supports the ban on the priesthood.
- Throughout the entire duration of the ban, Apostles supported the change as a revelation from the Lord.
- The growth of the Church and changing social conditions warranted changes in policy that made enforcement of the ban more difficult.[6]
- President Kimball was the first Church president to consider the historicity of the priesthood restriction and ask the Lord about the timing of removal.

Patience and Faith Tools
Identity Questions

- As I read the facts, which do I find most compelling?
- What facet is driving my questions and concerns?
- Which of my facets of identity most influence my interpretation of these facts?
- What facts would make the picture more complete? To what Identity do these data relate?

9 Tools of Knowing

1. Authoritarianism
2. Rationalism
3. Empiricism
4. Statistical Empiricism
5. Pragmatism
6. Skepticism
7. Conscience
8. Personal Revelation
9. Social Knowledge
    - What tools most heavily influence your understanding of this issue?
    - Which tools would help you improve your understanding of this issue?

---

6. Ibid., 16.

Ladder, Ripples, and the Rock

- Which of the facts provided takes you up the ladder most quickly?
- What information helps you question your assumptions?
- What facts do you automatically apply meaning?
- Which of the facts would you consider to be ripples?
- How do the ripples help you reconsider certain facts?
- Which facts appear to be built upon the rock?

WOMEN AND THE PRIESTHOOD

Facts and Information

- Men and women were created after the image of Heavenly Parents, male and female[7]
- Men and women possess inherit differences that complement one another.
- The keys of the Melchizedek Priesthood bestow the right of presidency, the right to administer in spiritual things, and the right to officiate in all of the offices of the Lord's Church (see D&C 107:8–9).
- For reasons not revealed, the Lord has established that men are to hold priesthood office in His Church.
- Since the Restoration, men and women of the Church in 1830 have understood that priesthood office is conferred upon men while the blessings of the priesthood are conferred jointly upon both men and women.[8]
- Only men who meet standards of worthiness are eligible for conferral of priesthood office.
- Men and women cannot be exalted without receiving and keeping the covenants associated with all ordinances of the Lord's house, including the new and everlasting covenant of marriage (see D&C 131:1–4).
- For reasons not revealed by the Lord, men must also receive the priesthood to enter the Lord's house and participate in temple ordinances.
- Men and women access the same priesthood power to magnify their callings and gain eternal life.

---

7. See "The Family: A Proclamation to the World," churchofjesuschrist.org; see also "Becoming Like God"; Elaine Anderson Cannon, "Mother in Heaven," in *Encyclopedia of Mormonism*, ed. Daniel H. Ludlow, 5 vols. (New York: Macmillan, 1992), 2:961. For an extensive survey of these teachings, see David L. Paulsen and Martin Pulido, "'A Mother There': A Survey of Historical Teachings about Mother in Heaven," *BYU Studies* 50, no. 1, 2011, 70–97.
8. See Gospel Topics Essays, "Joseph Smith's teaching on Priesthood, the Temple, and Women," footnotes 49–50.

- Both men and women exercise priesthood authority under the direction of priesthood keys.
- The Relief Society is the primary organization where women can give expression to many of their unique talents within the Lord's Church.
- Both men and women can receive spiritual gifts through faith in Christ and the gift of the Holy Ghost.
- Latter-day prophets have indicated that only priesthood holders may administer to the sick.[9]
- Church members follow Jesus's example and pray exclusively to our Father in Heaven.[10]

Patience and Faith Tools
Identity Questions

- As I read the facts, which do I find most compelling?
- What facet is driving my questions and concerns?
- Which of my facets of identity most influence my interpretation of these facts?
- What facts would make the picture more complete? To what Identity do these data relate?

9 Tools of Knowing

1. Authoritarianism
2. Rationalism
3. Empiricism
4. Statistical Empiricism
5. Pragmatism
6. Skepticism
7. Conscience
8. Personal Revelation
9. Social Knowledge
   - What tools most heavily influence your understanding of this issue?

---

9. *Handbook 2: Administering the Church*, 20.6.1.
10. 3 Nephi 18:19–21; Matthew 6:6–9; John 17:1, 5, 21, 24–25; see also Matthew 4:10; Luke 4:8; and 3 Nephi 13:9; 17:15.

- Which tools would help you improve your understanding of this issue?

Ladders, Ripples, and the Rock

- Which of the facts provided takes you up the ladder most quickly?
- What information helps you question your assumptions?
- What facts do you automatically apply meaning?
- Which of the facts would you consider to be ripples?
- How do the ripples help you reconsider certain facts?
- Which facts appear to be built upon the rock?

JOSEPH SMITH AND THE INSTITUTION OF PLURAL MARRIAGE[11]

Facts and Information

- The Lord revealed both the adoption and cessation of plural marriage.
- Knowledge about the doctrine of plural marriage was revealed to Joseph Smith as early as 1831.[12]
- Only two reasons for plural marriage are identified by the Lord in scripture (see Jacob 2:30; D&C 132:34–38).
- For both men and women who practiced plural marriage in Nauvoo, it was a difficult trial that challenged their notion of right and wrong.
- Joseph Smith shared the principle both with men he trusted and by revelation.
- Joseph Smith knew by revelation which women to approach.
- Women who were asked by Joseph to marry him were promised a witness from God that the principle was true, if they would accept the principle.[13]
- Joseph Smith was commanded to implement the principle but was never told how to do so.
- Joseph Smith knew the ramifications the practice would have upon his personal well-being and personal safety.
- Joseph Smith delayed fully implementing the practice because of concern for his wife Emma.[14]

---

11. See Gospel Topics Essays, "Plural Marriage in The Church of Jesus Christ of Latter-day Saints," https://www.churchofjesuschrist.org/study/manual/gospel-topics-essays/plural-marriage-in-the-church-of-jesus-christ-of-latter-day-saints?lang=eng.

12. See Andrew Jenson, "Plural Marriage," *Historical Record* 6 (May 1887): 232–33; "Report of Elders Orson Pratt and Joseph F. Smith," *Millennial Star* 40 (Dec. 16, 1878): 788; Daniel W. Bachman, "New Light on an Old Hypothesis: The Ohio Origins of the Revelation on Eternal Marriage," *Journal of Mormon History* 5, 1978, 19–32.

13. See Gospel Topics Essays, "Plural Marriage in The Church of Jesus Christ of Latter-day Saints," footnotes 36–37, 46–53.

14. R. Bushman, *Joseph Smith: Rough Stone Rolling* (New York: Knopf, 2005), 440.

- Joseph finally implemented the principle at the threat of angel.[15]
- Joseph Smith married between thirty and forty women during his lifetime, from fourteen to fifty-six years old.[16]
- Joseph Smith knowingly married some women who were already married to other men.
- Very few contemporary documents of the practice of plural marriage in Nauvoo exist; almost all accounts are later reminiscences.
- Joseph's motives for entering into plural marriage were primarily religious.
- Some of Joseph's plural marriages included sexual relationships and resulted in some children.[17]

Patience and Faith Tools
Identity Questions

- As I read the facts, which do I find most compelling?
- What facet is driving my questions and concerns?
- Which of my facets of identity most influence my interpretation of these facts?
- What facts would make the picture more complete? To what identity do these data relate?

9 Tools of Knowledge

1. Authoritarianism
2. Rationalism
3. Empiricism
4. Statistical Empiricism

---

15. See Brian C. Hales, "Encouraging Joseph Smith to Practice Plural Marriage: The Accounts of the Angel with a Drawn Sword," *Mormon Historical Studies* 11, no. 2 (Fall 2010): 69–70.
16. See Gospel Topics Essay: "Plural Marriage in The Church of Jesus Christ of Latter-day Saints," footnotes 25–28.
17. See Hales, *Joseph Smith's Polygamy*, 2:277–302. See Ugo A. Perego, "Joseph Smith, the Question of Polygamous Offspring, and DNA Analysis," in Newell G. Bringhurst and Craig L. Foster, eds., *The Persistence of Polygamy: Joseph Smith and the Origins of Mormon Polygamy* (Independence, MO: John Whitmer Books, 2010), 233–56.

5. Pragmatism
6. Skepticism
7. Conscience
8. Personal Revelation
9. Social Knowledge
   - What tools most heavily influence your understanding of this issue?
   - Which tools would help you improve your understanding of this issue?

Ladder, Ripples, and the Rock

- Which of the facts provided takes you up the ladder most quickly?
- What information helps you question your assumptions?
- What facts do you automatically apply meaning?
- Which of the facts would you consider to be ripples?
- How do the ripples help you reconsider certain facts?
- Which facts appear to be built upon the rock?

ORIGINS OF THE BOOK OF MORMON[18]

Facts and Information

- The translation of the Book of Mormon from physical plates is well documented and attested by multiple witnesses.
- Joseph Smith translated the plates through the Urim and Thummim and a stone called a seer stone.[19]
- Joseph Smith produced the record in less than sixty-five working days.
- Joseph Smith possessed limited schooling.
- No documentation or attestations from witnesses who participated in the translation of the Book of Mormon describe an alternative method of producing the Book of Mormon other than what Joseph described.
- Textual evidence from the original manuscript supports accounts of the those who participated in the process.
- The original manuscript underwent no essential revisions by Joseph Smith either during its production or prior to printing.
- Witnesses to the translation process are consistent in the following details:[20]

  - Joseph referred to no other manuscripts to develop the words.
  - The methods Joseph used to develop the words (looking into the Urim or Thummim or into a hat with a seer stone inside of it)
  - Spelling out of certain words
  - Verification of what was written
  - After breaks in transcribing, there was no read-back from the last place left off.
  - Joseph's general unawareness of certain details in the text that were later pointed out to him.
  - No reference to the physical plates during translation.

---

18. See Gospel Topics Essays, "Book of Mormon Translation," The Church of Jesus Christ of Latter-day Saints https://www.churchofjesuschrist.org/study/manual/gospel-topics-essays/book-of-mormon-translation?lang=eng.
19. Ibid. See footnotes 17 and 18.
20. Ibid. See footnotes 26–32.

- Joseph Smith provided no explanation for how he translated the Book of Mormon, only that it was done by the gift and power of God.[21]

Identity Questions

- As I read the facts, which do I find most compelling?
- What facet is driving my questions and concerns?
- Which of my facets of identity most influence my interpretation of these facts?
- What facts would make the picture more complete? To what identity do these data relate?

9 Tools of Knowledge

1. Authoritarianism
2. Rationalism
3. Empiricism
4. Statistical Empiricism
5. Pragmatism
6. Skepticism
7. Conscience
8. Personal Revelation
9. Social Knowledge
   - What tools most heavily influence your understanding of this issue?
   - Which tools would help you improve your understanding of this issue?

Ladder, Ripples, and the Rock

- Which of the facts provided takes you up the ladder most quickly?
- What information helps you question your assumptions?
- What facts do you automatically apply meaning?
- Which of the facts would you consider to be ripples?
- How do the ripples help you reconsider certain facts?
- Which facts appear to be built upon the rock?

---

21. See Preface to the Book of Mormon, 1830 edition.

THE BOOK OF ABRAHAM[22]

Facts and Information

- The Book of Abraham is accepted as scripture by The Church of Jesus Christ of Latter-day Saints.
- The Church makes no assertion that the Book of Abraham is contained on the remaining fragments of papyri.
- No eyewitness accounts of the translation of the Book of Abraham exist. However close observers who studied the papyri believe Joseph used the papyri to facilitate the reception of the Book of Abraham.[23]
- No statement from Joseph Smith exists on his methods used to produce the Book of Abraham.
- Many eyewitnesses saw the papyri from which Joseph Smith translated the book.
- Today, only a few small fragments remain of the papyri exist.
- Eyewitnesses attest and agree that the original scrolls were long and multiple, indicating more than what is in the Church's possession today.
- The relationship between the fragments of papyri we have today and those once in Joseph's possession is unclear.
- The Book of Abraham is consistent with other ancient texts about the life of Abraham and the ancient world.[24]
- The Book of Abraham teaches doctrines consistent with other scriptures and more clearly than those found in the Bible.
- Some manuscripts from Joseph Smith's history provide

---

22. See Gospel Topics Essays, "Translation and Historicity of the Book of Abraham," The Church of Jesus Christ of Latter-day Saints https://www.churchofjesuschrist.org/study/manual/gospel-topics-essays/translation-and-historicity-of-the-book-of-abraham?lang=eng.
23. See Gospel Topics Essays, footnotes 31–34.
24. See, for example, H. Nibley, *Abraham in Egypt* (Salt Lake City: Desert Book, 2000); J. Tvedtnes, B. Hauglid, and J. Gee, *Traditions About the Early Life of Abraham*, FARMS, 2001; D. Peterson, "News from Antiquity," *Ensign*, Jan. 1994, and J. Gee, "Research and Perspectives: Abraham in Ancient Egyptian Texts," *Ensign*, July 1992.

Egyptian characters followed by explanations.

- Explanations clearly aligned to Joseph Smith do not correspond to either the grammar or translation rules used by Egyptologists today.
- It is unclear what Joseph thought or believed about the remaining fragments of papyri as they are written by his scribes, namely W.W. Phelps.
- Existing papyri fragments date to the third century BCE and do not match the English text in the Book of Abraham.[25]

Identity Questions

- As I read the facts, which do I find most compelling?
- What facet is driving my questions and concerns?
- Which of my facets of identity most influence my interpretation of these facts?
- What facts would make the picture more complete? To what Identity do these data relate?

9 Tools of Knowing

1. Authoritarianism
2. Rationalism
3. Empiricism
4. Statistical Empiricism
5. Pragmatism
6. Skepticism
7. Conscience
8. Personal Revelation
9. Social Knowledge
   - What tools most heavily influence your understanding of this issue?
   - Which tools would help you improve your understanding of this issue?

---

25. See Gospel Topics Essays, footnotes 24–30.

Ladder, Ripples, and the Rock

- Which of the facts provided takes you up the ladder most quickly?
- What information helps you question your assumptions?
- What facts do you automatically apply meaning?
- Which of the facts would you consider to be ripples?
- How do the ripples help you reconsider certain facts?
- Which facts appear to be built upon the rock?

CONCLUSION

In this work I have tried to demonstrate that the best way to overcome the challenges of life is changing what we think by embracing fully the child of God identity. The child of God identity affects what we think, believe, and do because it changes how we see the world. It positions us to fully embrace our divine gift of agency and make choices that are more aligned to the truth that God has revealed for each of us.

Moreover, I have attempted to show that the child of God identity allows us to believe everything we want, while holding fast to all that the Lord has revealed. The child of God identity helps us deal with situations where the "why" of our beliefs have not fully been explained. Trusting in a few fundamentals that have been revealed by God as true can make all of the difference when facets of our identity pull us in conflicting directions from the strait and narrow path. The child of God identity gives us purpose to keep pressing forward in the midst of limited information.

Because our actions stem from what we believe, and our beliefs are influenced by how we see and interpret the information around us, I have also summarized nine tools of knowing that can make us better consumers of information. The nine tools of knowing provide clarity why we believe as we do, and help us scrutinize beliefs that we have held for a long time, but perhaps have run their course and should be discarded. Where the child of God identity initiates the process of deprioritizing long held beliefs that are incorrect, the nine tools of knowing can accelerate our inventorying of beliefs to leave behind. Each of us is in need of help on this front.

Revelation is a particular method of knowing that is vital to our survival in the latter days. Learning to distinguish between general revelations from prophets and apostles that require our support and allegiance—from other teachings that do not—is also essential. Fortunately, the Holy Ghost can give assurance of those things that the Lord would have us accept and support on a daily basis. Additionally, all general revelations have certain markers of authenticity that can be recognized by anyone anywhere. Knowing the markers of revelation from the Lord bring clarity to us when we encounter information that challenges our beliefs and actions.

Finally, repentance—the merciful process supplied by our merciful Redeemer—enables us to soften our hearts and minds so that they can be more easily changed. Changing our minds is really all that stands in our way of embracing the child of God identity and becoming sons and daughters of God completely—new creatures born again through the gospel of Jesus Christ. Our full potential lays before us, obstructed only by our former decisions governing our actions and beliefs that are contrary to the truth God has revealed. We can and must make changes here.

Embracing the child of God identity described in this work will do much to propel us forward towards our potential—our eternal potential—as President Nelson recently testified to an audience of young single adults: "I believe that if the Lord were speaking to you directly tonight, the first thing He would make sure you understand is your true identity. My dear friends, you are literally spirit children of God . . . first and foremost, each of you is a child of God."[1]

That you might come to fully embrace your divine identity as children of God, through an ongoing process of self-discovery and truth seeking—aided by the concepts and tools in this book—is my continual hope.

---

1. "Labels can be fun and indicate your support for any number of positive things. Many labels will change for you with the passage of time. And not all labels are of equal value. But if any label replaces your most important identifiers, the results can be spiritually suffocating. For example, if I were to rank in order of importance the designations that could be applied to me, I would say: First, I am a child of God—a son of God—then a son of the covenant, then a disciple of Jesus Christ and a devoted member of His restored church. Next would come my honored titles of husband and father, then Apostle of the Lord Jesus Christ. All other labels that have applied to me—such as medical doctor, surgeon, researcher, professor, lieutenant, captain, PhD, American, and so forth—would fall somewhere down the list" (R. Nelson, Worldwide Devotional for Young Adults in Salt Lake City, Utah, May 15, 2022. https://www.churchofjesuschrist.org/study/broadcasts/worldwide-devotional-for-young-adults/2022/05/12nelson?lang=eng).

APPENDIX A

Discovering Your Identity Worksheet

A few years ago, I asked my family at dinner, "After whom do you pattern your life?" If you reflect on that question a moment, you will discover that the person or persons look, sound, act, and think a lot like you! Now consider these questions: "Are they leading you where you want to go? What are the limitations of patterning your life in that way?" Use the worksheet on the following pages to sort through your many identities. Consider what you get from each of them and what they are costing you. Any identity not from God has limitations attached to them.

IDENTITY WORKSHEET

1. **Create a list of your many identities by completing the sentence, "I am . . ." Consider some of the contexts of your life (professional, family, country, and so on) to get you started. Some examples might include:**

"I am a Latter-day Saint."   "I am a lawyer."
"I am a mom."   "I am a (political party)."
"I am (gender identity)."   "I am a (nationality)."

_____   _____

_____   _____

_____   _____

_____   _____

_____   _____

_____   _____

2. **Rank order your list of identities from those that influence you most to least influential. Be as specific as possible. Those that elicit passion in your mind and heart are good indicators of which facets matter to you and are higher up in your hierarchy. Some additional questions to consider when making your identities include:**

   - What causes me outrage? To which identity does this belong? In what contexts do these issues show up?
   - What do you feel obligated—even compelled—to defend?
   - Which identities require beliefs or actions contrary to revealed doctrine through living prophets?
   - Which of your facets of identity are difficult to conceive as a decision? Some of these may be those that are the longest held, including nationality, race, gender, or familial relationships.

3. Reflect on your list. Ask yourself:

- Which identity was highest? Does my primary identity accurately describe what I think and feel as written, or does it need to be tailored further?
- What does that identity require of me to believe and do to be a full member?
- When did I choose that identity? Have I said "yes" to beliefs associated with that identity that I no longer mean?
- Which identities are higher/lower than expected? How are my beliefs and actions being affected by my primary identity?
- What do my facets of identity give me? What do I get from them that make it difficult to let go of them?
- How do my facets of identity enable and limit me?

INSPIRATIONS

_____

_____

_____

_____

_____

_____

_____

_____

_____

_____

ABOUT THE AUTHOR

Joshua L. Savage earned his doctorate in organizational change and leadership from the University of Southern California. He has worked in a variety of industries as a change and transformation expert. He currently works as the director of organization development for Intel, helping leaders transform their business by thinking differently.

Dr. Savage is the author of several books, including *Renewing Your Relationship with Jesus*. He and his wife are the parents of four children and currently reside in Gilbert, Arizona.